THE EYE

THE PHYSIOLOGY OF HUMAN PERCEPTION

THE HUMAN BODY

THE EYE

THE PHYSIOLOGY
OF HUMAN PERCEPTION

EDITED BY KARA ROGERS, SENIOR EDITOR, BIOMEDICAL SCIENCES

Britannica®
Educational Publishing

IN ASSOCIATION WITH

ROSEN
EDUCATIONAL SERVICES

Published in 2011 by Britannica Educational Publishing
(a trademark of Encyclopædia Britannica, Inc.)
in association with Rosen Educational Services, LLC
29 East 21st Street, New York, NY 10010.

First Edition

Britannica Educational Publishing
Michael I. Levy: Executive Editor
J.E. Luebering: Senior Manager
Marilyn L. Barton: Senior Coordinator, Production Control
Steven Bosco: Director, Editorial Technologies
Lisa S. Braucher: Senior Producer and Data Editor
Yvette Charboneau: Senior Copy Editor
Kathy Nakamura: Manager, Media Acquisition
Kara Rogers: Senior Editor, Biomedical Sciences

Rosen Educational Services
Alexandra Hanson-Harding: Senior Editor
Nelson Sá: Art Director
Cindy Reiman: Photography Manager
Matthew Cauli: Designer, Cover Design
Introduction by Sean Price

Library of Congress Cataloging-in-Publication Data

The eye : the physiology of human perception / edited by Kara Rogers. — 1st ed.
   p. cm. — (The human body)
"In association with Britannica Educational Publishing, Rosen Educational Services."
Includes bibliographical references and index.
ISBN 978-1-61530-116-4 (lib. bdg.)
1. Eye—Popular works. 2. Perception—Physiological aspects—Popular works. I. Rogers, Kara.
QP475.5.E94 2010
612.8'4—dc22

2009051116

Manufactured in the United States of America

On the cover: *The adult human eye is only 24 mm (1 inch) high and slightly wider. This organ receives an astonishing amount of information and conveys it to the brain for processing.* © www.istockphoto.com / Mads Abildgaard (head), Nurbek Sagynbaev (eye)

Introduction: *Patient being fitted for glasses by an eye specialist.* Shutterstock.com

CONTENTS

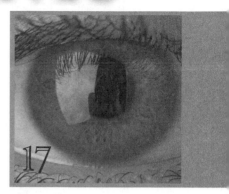

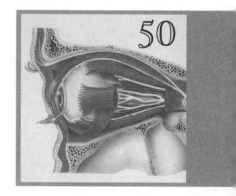

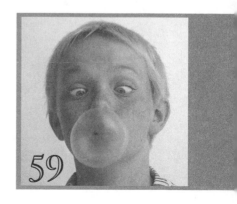

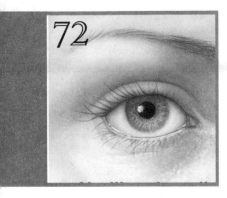

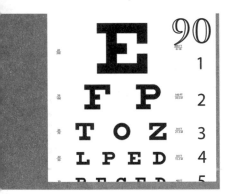

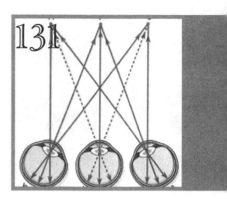

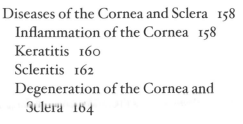

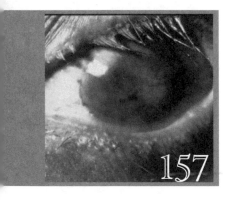

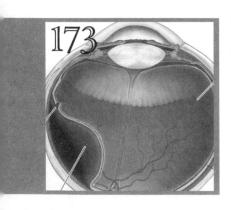

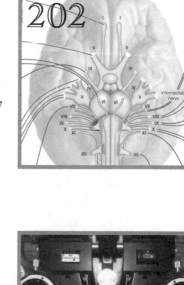

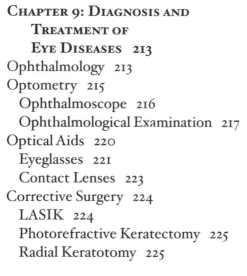

INTRODUCTION

The scientific study of the eye is believed to have originated with the Greek physician Herophilus, who lived from about 335 to 280 BCE. Indeed, from his work came the words that we use today to describe the various parts of the eye, including the words *retina* and *cornea*. In Herophilus' day, scientists believed that we could see because beams of light came out of our eyes and fixed on objects. In the centuries since, doctors and anatomists have discovered that vision relies on just the opposite effect. Human eyes are actually light collectors. Light rays travel from objects around us and stimulate the light-sensitive cells in our eyes. This book takes a look at these amazing organs and how they function to allow us to see the world.

Anyone staring into another person's eye would notice that its exterior is mostly white. This part of the human eye, the sclera, is made up of fibrous tissue and provides a tough protective coating around the whole eyeball. The most noticeable part of any eye is the coloured iris and the dark pupil that it surrounds. The iris, which works much like the aperture of a camera, expands in darkness to let more light into the pupil and contracts in bright light to keep the light-sensitive cells from being overwhelmed. The colour of the iris comes from melanin, a substance that protects the eye from absorbing strong light. In the centre of the iris is the pupil, which allows light and other visual information into the interior of the eye. The iris and pupil are protected by a transparent, domelike cover called the cornea.

Light enters the interior of the eye by passing through a crystalline lens, which bulges or flattens, depending on how far away an image is, and then through a semisolid gel-filled chamber called the vitreous body. The vitreous body gives the eye shape and flexibility. Finally, the light reaches the retina, a membrane made up of layers of cells, which receive visual information and transmit this information to the brain.

The eyes would not be able to receive this information if they did not move. How they move is a complicated process. Eyeballs are set into protected parts of the skull called eye sockets. Between the sockets and the eyeballs are layers of fat and six thin muscles that gently tug the eyeball in one direction or another. Most of the actual movements of the eyes are carried out without awareness. For example, when a person sees bright light at the edge of the field of vision, he or she is immediately drawn to look at it. This response is called the fixation reflex. Scientists have also learned that the eyes move a number of times within a single second. These tiny movements help keep the eyes focused on a world that is constantly in motion and stimulate the retina to take in fresh visual information even with stationary objects.

Eyes are delicate and precise organs that are vulnerable to problems. There are, however, a number of mechanisms in place to protect the eyes. Eyebrows and eyelashes keep out dust, sweat, and other irritants. Eyelids lubricate the surface of the eyeball and protect against the introduction of foreign bodies into the eye. Lacrimal glands at the outside upper corner of each eye create a steady supply of tears to keep the eyeballs moist. Tears— produced by irritation, yawning, and crying—also contain bacteria-killing enzymes that destroy infections. To keep the eyes moist, we blink, often involuntarily.

The retina in the back of the eye has an especially valuable role to play in vision. Light-sensitive cells in the retina, known as rods and cones because of their distinctive shapes, enable us to see. For example, cones are highly sensitive to colour, and thus they are responsible for daylight (photopic) colour vision and for fine visual discrimination. Most of them are concentrated around a small dimple in a part of the retina called the fovea, or macula lutea.

In the darkness of night, the light-sensing rods are far more helpful than the cone cells. Rods are responsible for motion detection and for night (scotopic) vision. After 30 minutes in the dark, the human eye can become up to 10,000 times more sensitive to light. Night vision is also different from day vision because the cones are much less active, resulting in reduced detection of colour.

As cones and rods react to stimuli, they excite nerve-cell bodies called ganglions. Ganglion cells send this raw information to the brain, which then translates it into a visual image. Scientists have learned much about vision through studying the electrophysiology of the retina. Many studies have focused primarily on what happens when the eyes are electrically stimulated. By placing an electrode on the eye, scientists can create electroretinograms, which show the electrical impulses that enable the eyes to communicate with the brain. These types of studies have helped scientists to identify and understand new information concerning the electrical pathways of the rods and cones. Such studies have also greatly expanded scientists' understanding of how people perceive colour. Colour blindness, inherited forms of which commonly affect males, occurs because the colour-sensitive cones in a person's retinas are missing or weak. Because in many cases only certain cones are affected, colour-blind persons usually can see at least some colour. For instance, a person whose red cones are missing or do not work cannot distinguish between red and green.

When light projects an image onto the retina in the back of the eye, the image is upside down, reversed (with respect to left and right), and two-dimensional. The optic nerve sends this image to the back of the brain, to an area called the occipital lobe. Fortunately, the brain knows how to translate this image into one that is right side up and non-reversed. Also, the image appears three-dimensional because the separation of the two eyes enables each eye to see an object from a slightly different angle. The brain takes the two retinas' information and fuses it into a single three-dimensional image through a process called stereoscopic focus. How the eyes work together and coordinate two sets of images is a complex topic, one that is explored in this volume.

In the 20th and early 21st centuries, a significant amount of information about the human eye was gleaned from studies of eye disease. Malfunction of the eyes and of the visual process has helped scientists to understand the basic structures of the eye and how each structure contributes to vision.

Diseases and other eye problems can take place within different parts of the eye. Some of the ailments of the outer eye include sty, an inflammation of the eyelid, and trachoma, a bacterial disease that is prevalent in poverty-stricken areas of the world. The eyelashes of trachoma victims turn inward and brush against the corneas. This constant irritation can scar the cornea. Inner eye diseases include problems such as cataracts. In persons with cataracts, the lenses of the eyes lose their transparency and appear to have a milky cover. Cataracts can be caused by birth defects, wounds, exposure to X-rays, drugs, or old age. In many cases, cataracts can be corrected by surgery.

There are a variety of conditions that can affect the retina. For example, the retina can become detached from the underlying layer of supporting cells called the retinal pigment epithelium. Retinal detachment can cause "floaters"—deposits in the eye that produce visual spots or shadows. Sometimes retinal detachment is caused by trauma, but more often it is caused by aging and changes of the gel in the vitreous body. Macular degeneration is a blinding disorder that is characterized by the gradual deterioration of the retina, particularly the fovea. Persons with macular degeneration sometimes have blind spots in the centre of the visual field before they lose their sight entirely. Premature babies are sometimes treated with oxygen in order to help them survive their first days of life. This excess oxygen, however, can cause the infants' retinal blood vessels to develop abnormally, giving rise to a condition known as retinopathy of prematurity, which can lead to blindness.

Accidents are another important cause of blindness. Mishaps with household chemicals or even looking at the sun too long can destroy vision. In addition, there are a number of abnormalities, including nearsightedness (seeing only close objects clearly), farsightedness (seeing only distant objects clearly), and astigmatism (in which all objects are blurry), that can result in impaired vision.

Since the 1200s, physicians have been able to correct ordinary vision problems like nearsightedness and farsightedness. Reading glasses were first used in Europe and China, but they remained expensive and rare. In the 1780s, Benjamin Franklin became frustrated by repeatedly having to take off his reading glasses and put on a different pair of glasses when he needed to see at a distance. As a result, Franklin inserted distance lenses in the top half of his eyeglass frames and reading lenses in the bottom half, thereby creating the first bifocals.

But it was German scientist Hermann von Helmholtz who developed the modern field of ophthalmology. He did it by inventing the ophthalmoscope, which allows doctors to see inside the eye. Thanks to the pioneering efforts of Helmholtz and others, there are now three different types of eye specialists: ophthalmologists, medical doctors who focus on eye problems and perform surgery; optometrists, who give eye exams and prescribe corrective lenses; and opticians, who fit, supply, and adjust eyewear for patients.

Painter and inventor Leonardo da Vinci came up with the idea of contact lenses in 1508. But it wasn't until 1887 that the first contacts were actually produced. These glass lenses were so large and uncomfortable that they could be worn only for an hour at a time. The first practical contact lenses did not come along until 1938. But these rigid plastic contacts remained uncomfortable for most people. Finally, in the 1970s, scientists introduced "soft" contacts made of flexible plastic.

Starting in the 1990s, people began turning to eye surgery to permanently correct nearsightedness, farsightedness, and astigmatism. LASIK (laser-assisted in situ keratomileusis) surgery has become popular. In this procedure, doctors cut a tiny flap across the clear cornea and fold it back so that a laser can then reshape the tissue underneath. In the mid-2000s, roughly 1.4 million people a year underwent this type of surgery.

By studying the human eye, medical experts have learned not only about the eye itself but also about the way the brain functions as we look out onto the world. As science moves forward, researchers are discovering new ways to treat and cure eye diseases and disorders, giving many persons affected by such conditions the gift of vision. This book will allow readers to see the human eye in a new way.

CHAPTER 1
ANATOMY OF THE EYE

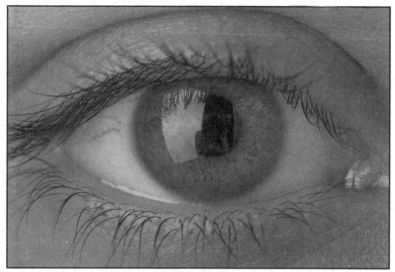

Close-up of a human eye. Shutterstock.com

The human eye is an amazingly complex structure that enables sight, one of the most important of the human senses. Sight underlies our ability to understand the world around us and to navigate within our environment. As we look at the world around us, our eyes are constantly taking in light, a component fundamental to the visual process. The front of the human eye contains a curved lens, through which light reflected from objects in the surrounding environment passes. The light travels deep into the eyeball, passing all the way to the back of the eye, where it converges to a point. A unique set of cells at the back of the eye receives the light, harnessing its energy by converting it into an electrical impulse, or signal, that then travels along neurons in the brain. The impulses are carried along a neuronal pathway that extends from the back of the eye all the way to the back of the brain, ultimately terminating in a region known as the visual cortex. There, the electrical signals from both eyes are processed and unified into a single image. The amount of time between the moment when light enters the eye and when a unified image is generated in the brain is near instantaneous, taking only fractions of a second.

Scientists' knowledge of the intricacy and the complex associations of the vital structures within the human eye expanded tremendously in the 20th and early 21st centuries. Although some of this knowledge was obtained from studies of the eyes of animals, a significant amount of information was also gained from studies of diseases of the human eye. With this knowledge came an understanding of the function of each of the eye structures. Each structure contributes in a specific way to the visual process, and collectively they underlie a broad range of visual functions, from the perception of an object's shape, size, and colour to the perception of distance.

THE EYE

The eyeball can be viewed as the fusing together of a small portion of a small, strongly curved sphere with a large portion of a large, not so strongly curved sphere. The small piece, occupying about one-sixth of the whole, has a radius of 8 mm (0.3 inch); it is transparent and is called the cornea; the remainder, called the scleral segment, is opaque and has a radius of 12 mm (0.5 inch). The ring where the two areas join is called the limbus. Thus, on looking directly into the eye from in front one sees the white sclera surrounding the cornea; because the latter is transparent one sees, instead of the cornea, a ring of tissue lying within the eye, the iris. The iris is the structure that determines the colour of the eye. The centre of this ring is called the pupil. It appears dark because the light passing into the eye is not reflected back to any great extent. By use of an ophthalmoscope, an instrument that permits the observer to illuminate the interior of the eyeball while observing through the pupil, the appearance of the interior lining of the globe can be made out. The lining, called the fundus oculi, is characterized by the large blood vessels that supply blood to the retina; these are especially distinct as they cross over the pale optic disk, or papilla, the region where the optic nerve fibres leave the globe.

The dimensions of the eye are reasonably constant, varying among healthy individuals by only a millimetre or two; the sagittal (vertical) diameter is about 24 mm (about 1 inch) and is usually less than the transverse (horizontal) diameter. At birth the sagittal diameter is about 16 to 17 mm (about 0.65 inch); it increases rapidly to about 22.5 to 23 mm (about 0.89 inch) by age 3; between ages 3 and 13 the globe attains its full size. The weight is about 7.5 grams (0.25 ounce), and its volume 6.5 mm (0.4 cubic inch).

The eye is made up of three coats, which enclose the optically clear aqueous humour, lens, and vitreous body. The outermost coat consists of the cornea and the sclera; the middle coat, or uvea, contains the main blood supply to the eye and consists, from the back forward, of the choroid, the ciliary body, and the iris. The innermost layer is the retina, lying on the choroid and receiving most of its nourishment from the vessels within the choroid, the remainder of its nourishment being derived from the retinal vessels that lie on its surface and are visible in the ophthalmoscope. The ciliary body and iris have a very thin covering, the ciliary epithelium and posterior epithelium of the iris, which is continuous with the retina.

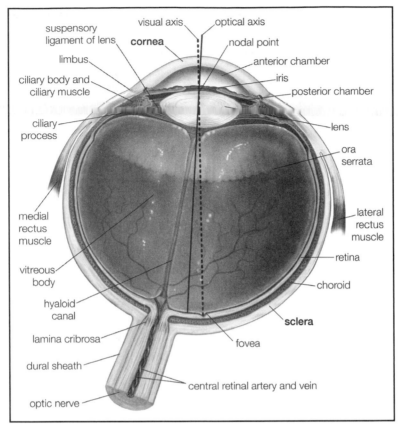

Horizontal cross section of the human eye, showing the structures of the eye, the visual axis (the central point of image focusing in the retina), and the optical axis (the axis about which the eye is rotated by the eye muscles).
Encyclopædia Britannica, Inc.

Within the cavities formed by this triple-layered coat there are the crystalline lens, suspended by fine transparent fibres—the suspensory ligament or zonule of Zinn—from the ciliary body; the aqueous humour, a clear fluid filling the spaces between the cornea and the lens and iris; and the vitreous body, a clear jelly filling the much larger cavity enclosed by the sclera, the ciliary body, and the lens. The anterior chamber of the eye is defined as the space between the cornea and the forward surfaces of the iris and lens, while the posterior chamber is the much smaller space between the rear surface of the iris and the ciliary body, zonule, and lens; the two chambers both contain aqueous humour and are in connection through the pupil. This connection allows the aqueous humour to flow through the pupil from the posterior chamber to the anterior chamber. From there, the fluid flows out of the eye through the trabecular meshwork and Schlemm's canal, which encircles the peripheral iris. Some aqueous humour also exits the eye directly through the ciliary body. The ciliary muscle attachments and the lens separate the aqueous humour in front from the vitreous humour behind.

The eye also contains special light receptors, called photoreceptors, and its construction is much like that of a simple camera. The retina, an extremely metabolically active layer of nerve tissue, is made up of millions of photoreceptors. Various structures of the eye function to focus light onto the retina, with the cornea providing the greatest focusing power of the eye. The cornea is curved to a much greater extent than the rest of the eyeball. However, the shape and focusing power of the cornea are not adjustable. This is in contrast to the lens, the shape of which is adjustable and is controlled by the action of the ciliary body, altering the focusing power of the lens as needed. The cornea and lens focus an image onto the retina at the back of the eye. If the image is projected too far in front of the retina, it causes the visual defect called myopia, or nearsightedness. If the image is theoretically focused "behind" the retina, the result is hyperopia, or farsightedness. If no deformation of the lens is present, the image is projected onto the fovea, a structure near the centre of the retina that contains a large number of cone photoreceptors and that provides the sharpest vision. When stimulated by light, retinal photoreceptor cells send signals to neighbouring cells in the retina that then relay the signals through the optic nerve to the visual centres of the brain.

OUTER TISSUES OF THE EYEBALL

The outermost coat of the eye is made up of the cornea and the sclera. Though these two structures are essentially extensions of the same layer of tissue in the eye, they have distinct functions, with the cornea playing a vital role in focusing light for photoreception and the sclera fulfilling an important role in the protection of the eyeball.

CORNEA

The cornea is the transparent window of the eye. It is about 12 mm (0.5 inch) in diameter and, except at its margins, contains no blood vessels. However, it does contain many nerves and is very sensitive to pain or touch. It is nourished and provided with oxygen anteriorly by tears and is bathed posteriorly by aqueous humour. It protects the pupil, the iris, and the inside of the eye from penetration by foreign bodies and is the first and most powerful element in the eye's focusing system. As light passes through the cornea, it is partially refracted before reaching the lens. The curvature of the cornea, which is spherical in infancy but changes with age, gives it its focusing power; when the curve becomes irregular, it causes a focusing defect called astigmatism, in which images appear elongated or distorted.

The cornea contains five distinguishable layers: the epithelium, or outer covering; Bowman's membrane; the stroma, or supporting structure; Descemet's membrane; and the endothelium, or inner lining. Up to 90 percent of the thickness of the cornea is made up of the stroma. The epithelium, which is a continuation of the epithelium of the conjunctiva, is itself made up of about six layers of cells. The superficial layer is continuously being shed, and the layers are renewed by multiplication of the cells in the innermost, or basal, layer.

The stroma appears as a set of lamellae, or plates, running parallel with the surface and superimposed on each other like the leaves of a book; between the lamellae lie the corneal corpuscles, cells that synthesize new collagen (connective tissue protein) essential for the repair and maintenance of this layer. The lamellae are made up of microscopically visible fibres that run parallel to form sheets; in successive lamellae the fibres make a large angle with each other. The lamellae in humans are about 1.5 to 2.5 micrometres (1 micrometre = 0.001 millimetre) thick, so that there are about 200 lamellae in the human cornea. The fibrous basis of the stroma is collagen.

Immediately above the stroma, adjacent to the epithelium, is Bowman's membrane, about 8 to 14 micrometres thick; with the electron microscope it is evident that it is really stroma, but with the collagen fibrils not arranged in the orderly fashion seen in the rest of the stroma.

Beneath the stroma are Descemet's membrane and the endothelium. The former is about 5 to 10 micrometres thick and is made up of a different type of collagen from that in the stroma; it is secreted by the cells of the endothelium, which is a single layer of flattened cells. There is apparently no continuous renewal of these cells as with the epithelium, so that damage to this layer is a more serious matter.

The most obvious difference between the opaque sclera and the transparent cornea is the irregularity in the sizes and arrangement of the collagen fibrils in the sclera by contrast with the almost uniform thickness and strictly parallel array in the cornea; in addition, the cornea has a much higher percentage of mucopolysaccharide (a carbohydrate that has among its repeating units a nitrogenous sugar, hexosamine) as embedding material for the collagen fibrils. It has been shown that the regular arrangement of the fibrils is, in fact, the essential factor leading to the transparency of the cornea.

When the cornea is damaged—e.g., by a virus infection—the collagen laid down in the repair processes is not regularly arranged, with the result that an opaque patch called a leukoma, may occur. When an eye is removed or a person dies, the cornea soon loses its transparency, becoming hazy; this is due to the taking in of fluid from the aqueous humour, the cornea becoming thicker as it becomes hazier. The cornea can be made to reassume its transparency by maintaining it in a warm, well-aerated chamber, at about 31 °C (88 °F, its normal temperature); associated with this return of transparency is a loss of fluid.

The innermost layer of the cornea, the endothelium, plays a critical role in keeping the cornea from becoming swollen with excess fluid. Under normal conditions, the cornea tends to take in fluid and solutes, mainly from the aqueous humour and from the small blood vessels at the limbus. This is counteracted by the active transport of solutes from the cornea, which results in the movement of fluid from the cornea via osmotic gradients. The active transport of solutes depends on an adequate supply of energy, and any situation that prejudices this supply causes the cornea to swell—transport fails, or works so slowly that it cannot remove solutes and fluid as quickly as they enter.

When endothelial cells are lost, new cells are not produced; rather, existing cells expand to fill in the space left behind. Once loss of a critical number of endothelial cells has occurred, however, active transport of solutes decreases or becomes impaired. As a result, the cornea swells, causing decreased vision and, in severe cases, surface changes and pain. Endothelial cell loss can be accelerated via mechanical trauma or abnormal age-related endothelial cell death (called Fuchs endothelial dystrophy). Death of the eye causes complete transport failure, primarily because of the loss of temperature; if the dead eye is placed in a warm chamber, the reserves of metabolic energy it contains in the form of sugar and glycogen are adequate to keep the cornea transparent for 24 hours or more. When it is required to store corneas for grafting, as in an eye bank, the cornea is removed from the globe to prevent it from absorbing fluid from the aqueous humour.

The cornea is exquisitely sensitive to pain; for example, a corneal abrasion, or scratch, most often causes a sensation of something being on the eye and is accompanied by intense tearing, pain, and light sensitivity. The sensation of pain in the cornea is mediated by sensory nerve fibres, called ciliary nerves, that run just underneath the endothelium; they belong to the ophthalmic branch of the fifth cranial nerve, the large sensory nerve of the head. The ciliary nerves leave the globe through openings in the sclera, not in company with the optic nerve, which is concerned exclusively with responses of the retina to light.

The sclera is essentially the continuation backward of the cornea, the collagen fibres of the cornea being, in effect, continuous with those of the sclera. The sclera is pierced by numerous nerves and blood vessels; the largest of these holes is that formed by the optic nerve, the posterior scleral foramen. The outer two-thirds of the sclera in this region continue backward along the nerve to blend with its covering, or dural sheath—in fact, the sclera may be regarded as a continuation of the dura mater, the outer covering of the brain. The inner third of the sclera, combined with some choroidal tissue, stretches across the opening, and the sheet thus formed is perforated to permit the passage of fasciculi (bundles of fibres) of the optic nerve. This region is called the lamina cribrosa. The blood vessels of the sclera are largely confined to a superficial layer of tissue, and these, along with the conjunctival vessels, are responsible for the bright redness of the inflamed eye. As with the cornea, the innermost layer is a single layer of endothelial cells; above this is the lamina fusca, characterized by large numbers of pigment cells.

Uveal Tract

The middle coat of the eye is called the uvea (from the Latin for "grape") because the eye looks like a reddish-blue grape when the outer coat has been dissected away. The posterior part of the uvea, the choroid, is essentially a layer of blood vessels and connective tissue sandwiched between the sclera and the retina. The forward portion of the uvea, the ciliary body and iris, is more complex, containing as it does the ciliary muscle and the sphincter and dilator of the pupil.

The blood supply responsible for nourishing the retina consists of the retinal and uveal circulations, both of which derive from branches of the ophthalmic artery. The two systems of blood vessels differ in that the retinal vessels, which supply nutrition to the innermost layers of the retina, derive from a branch of the ophthalmic artery, called the central artery of the retina, that enters the eye with the optic nerve, while the uveal circulation, which supplies the middle and outer layers of the retina as well as the uvea, is derived from branches of the ophthalmic artery that penetrate the globe independently of the optic nerve.

The ciliary body is the forward continuation of the choroid. It is a muscular ring, triangular in horizontal section, beginning at the region called the ora serrata and ending, in front, as the root of the iris. The surface is thrown into folds, called ciliary processes, the whole being covered by the ciliary epithelium, which is a double layer of cells; the layer next to the vitreous body, called the inner layer, is transparent, while the outer layer, which is continuous with the pigment epithelium of the retina, is heavily pigmented. These two layers are to be regarded embryologically as the forward continuation of the retina, which terminates at the ora serrata. Their function is to secrete the aqueous humour.

The ciliary muscle is an unstriped, involuntary, muscle concerned with alterations in the adjustments of focus — accommodation — of the optical system; the fibres run both across the muscle ring and circularly, and the effect of their contraction is to cause the whole body to move forward and to become fatter, so that the suspensory ligament that holds the lens in place is loosened.

Iris

The most anterior portion of the uvea is the iris. This is the only portion that is visible to superficial inspection, appearing as a perforated disc, the central perforation, or pupil, varying in size according to the surrounding illumination and other factors. A prominent feature is the collarette at the inner edge, representing the place of attachment of the embryonic pupillary membrane that, in embryonic life, covers the pupil. As with the ciliary body, with which it is anatomically continuous, the iris consists of several layers: namely, an anterior layer of endothelium, the stroma; and the posterior iris epithelium. The stroma contains the blood vessels and the two sheets of smooth muscle, the sphincter and dilator muscles, that control the contraction (constriction) and the expansion (dilation) of the iris, respectively. In addition, the stroma contains pigment cells that determine the colour of the eye.

Posteriorly, the stroma is covered by a double layer of epithelium, the continuation forward of the ciliary epithelium; here, however, both layers are heavily pigmented and serve to prevent light from passing through the iris tissue, confining the optical pathway to the pupil. The pink iris of the albino is the result of the absence of pigment in these layers. The cells of the anterior layer of the iris epithelium have projections that become the fibres of the dilator muscle; these projections run radially, so that when they contract they pull the iris into folds and widen the pupil; by contrast, the fibres of the sphincter pupillae muscle run in a circle around the pupil, so that when they contract the pupil becomes smaller. By controlling the size of the pupil, these muscles determine how much light reaches the sensory tissue of the retina, which is important for optimal vision. Thus, in bright light, the sphincter muscle constricts, whereas in low light or darkness, the dilator muscle expands the opening.

Eyes that are the colour blue may result from decreased amounts of pigment in the stroma; the light reflected back from the posterior epithelium, which is blue because of scattering and selective absorption, passes through the stroma to the eye of the observer. As time goes on, pigment may be deposited, and the colour may change; thus, if much pigment is laid down the eye becomes brown or black, if little, it remains blue or gray.

Inflammation of the iris is termed iritis or anterior uveitis, a condition that commonly has no determinable cause. As a result of inflammation, the iris sticks to the lens or the cornea, blocking the normal flow of fluid in the eye. Complications of iritis include secondary glaucoma and blindness; treatment usually involves topical steroid eyedrops.

Pupil

Light must pass through the pupil before it can reach the lens and be focused onto the retina. Parasympathetic nerve fibres from the third (oculomotor) cranial nerve innervate the muscle of the iris that causes constriction of the pupil, whereas sympathetic nerve fibres control dilation. The pupillary aperture also narrows when focusing on close objects and dilates for more distant viewing. At its maximum contraction, the adult pupil may be less than 1 mm (0.04 inch) in diameter, and it may increase up to 10 times to its maximum diameter. The size of the human pupil may also vary as a result of age, disease, trauma, or other abnormalities within the visual system, including dysfunction of the pathways controlling pupillary movement. Thus, careful evaluation of the pupils is an important part of both eye and neurologic exams.

Dilator Muscle

The dilator muscle of the iris involuntarily contracts as available light decreases, thus dilating the pupil. Pupillary dilation is controlled primarily by the sympathetic nervous system. Interruption of the innervation of the dilator muscle can cause an abnormally small pupil, a condition seen as part of Horner syndrome. Traumatic rupture of iris muscles can cause an irregularly shaped pupil. Dilator muscles can also be found in other parts of the body such as the nose, where the dilator naris muscle aids in widening the nostrils.

INNER TISSUES OF THE EYEBALL

PIGMENTED EPITHELIUM

Separating the choroid (the middle tunic of the globe, or eyeball) from the retina proper is a layer of pigmented cells, known as the pigment epithelium. This layer of the retina acts as a restraining barrier to the indiscriminate diffusion of material from the blood in the choroid to the retina. The retina ends at the ora serrata, where the ciliary body begins. The pigment epithelium continues forward as a pigmented layer of cells covering the ciliary body; farther forward still, the epithelium covers the posterior surface of the iris and provides the cells that constitute the dilator muscle of this diaphragm. Next to the pigment epithelium of the retina is the neuroepithelium, or rods and cones. Their continuation forward is represented by a second layer of epithelial cells covering the ciliary body; the term *ciliary epithelium* is used to describe the two layers of cells that are the embryological equivalent of the retinal pigment epithelium and the receptor layer (rods and cones) of the retina. The unpigmented layer of the ciliary epithelium is continued forward over the back of the iris, where it acquires pigment and is called the posterior iris epithelium.

THE RETINA

The retina is a layer of nervous tissue that covers the inside of the back two-thirds of the eyeball, in which stimulation by light occurs, initiating the sensation of vision. The retina is actually an extension of the brain, formed embryonically from neural tissue and connected to the brain proper by the optic nerve. The retina functions specifically to receive light and to convert it into chemical energy. The chemical energy activates nerves that conduct the electrical messages out of the eye into the higher regions of the brain.

Ten layers of cells in the retina can be seen microscopically. In general, there are four main layers: (1) Next to the choroid is the pigment epithelium. (2) Above the epithelium is the layer of rods and cones, the light-sensitive cells. The changes induced in the rods and cones by light are transmitted to (3) a layer of neurons (nerve cells) called the bipolar cells. These bipolar cells connect with (4) the innermost layer of neurons, the ganglion cells; and the transmitted messages are carried out of the eye along their projections, or axons, which constitute the optic nerve fibres. Thus, the optic nerve is really a central tract, rather than a nerve, connecting two regions of the nervous system, namely, the layer of bipolar cells, and the cells of the lateral geniculate body, the latter being a visual relay station in the diencephalon (the rear portion of the forebrain).

The arrangement of the retinal cells in an orderly manner gives rise to the outer nuclear layer, containing the nuclei of the rods and cones; the inner nuclear layer, containing the nuclei and perikarya (main cell bodies outside the nucleus) of the bipolar cells, and the ganglion cell layer, containing the corresponding structures of the ganglion cells. The plexiform layers are regions in which the neurons make their interconnections. Thus, the outer plexiform layer contains the rod and cone projections terminating as the rod spherule and cone pedicle; these make connections with the dendritic processes of the bipolar cells, so that changes produced by light in the rods and cones are transmitted by way of these connections to the bipolar cells. (The dendritic process of a nerve cell is the projection that receives nerve impulses to the cell; the axon is the projection that carries impulses from the cell.) In the inner plexiform layer are the axons of the bipolar cells and the dendritic processes of the ganglion and amacrine cells (the latter are neurons lacking long axons, instead possessing shorter axon-like projections that relay signals to ganglion cells). The association is such as to allow messages in the bipolar cells to be transmitted to the ganglion cells, the messages then passing out along the axons of the ganglion cells as optic nerve messages.

The photosensitive cells, or photoreceptors, are of two kinds, called rods and cones, the rods being usually much thinner than the cones but both being built up on the same plan. The light-sensitive pigment is contained in the outer segment, which rests on the pigment epithelium. Through the other end, called the synaptic body, effects of light are transmitted to the bipolar cells and to the horizontal cells of the outer plexiform layer. When examined in the electron microscope, the outer segments of the rods and cones are seen to be composed of stacks of disks, apparently made by the infolding of the limiting membrane surrounding the outer segment; the visual pigment, located on the surfaces of these disks, is thus spread over a very wide area, and this contributes to the efficiency with which light is absorbed by the visual cell.

When light enters the eye, it passes through the cornea and the lens and is refracted, focusing an image onto the retina. Thus, light must first pass through light-insensitive layers before it reaches the light-sensitive rods and cones. The optical disadvantages of this arrangement are largely overcome by the development of the fovea centralis, a localized region of the retina, close to the optic axis of the eye, where the inner layers of the retina are absent. The result is a depression, the foveal pit, where light has an almost unrestricted passage to the light-sensitive cells. It is essentially this region of the retina that is employed for accurate vision, the eyes being directed toward the objects of regard so that their images fall in this restricted region. If the object of interest is large, so as to subtend a large angle, then the eye must move rapidly from region to region so as to bring their images successively onto the fovea; this is typically seen during reading.

In the central region of the fovea there are cones exclusively; toward its edges, rods also occur, and as successive zones are reached the proportion of rods increases while the absolute density of packing of the receptors tends to decrease. Thus, the central fovea is characterized by an exclusive population of very densely packed cones; here, also, the cones are very thin and in form very similar to rods. The region surrounding the fovea is called the parafovea; it stretches about 1,250 micrometres from the centre of the fovea, and it is here that the highest density of rods occurs. Surrounding the parafovea, in turn, is the perifovea, its outermost edge being 2,750 micrometres from the centre of the fovea; here the density of cones is still further diminished, the number being only 12 per 100 micrometres compared with 50 per 100 micrometres in the most central region of the fovea. In the whole human retina there are said to be about 7,000,000 cones and from 75,000,000 to 150,000,000 rods. Rods predominate in nocturnal animals and are most sensitive to reduced light intensities; in humans they provide night vision and aid in visual orientation. Cones are more prominent in humans and those animals that are active during the day and provide detailed vision (as for reading) and colour perception. In general, the more cones per unit area of retina, the finer the detail that can be discriminated by that area.

The fovea is sometimes referred to as the macula lutea ("yellow spot"), a circular patch of tissue about 5 to 6 mm (0.2 to 0.24 inch) in diameter. The macula lutea is a rather vague area, characterized by the presence of a yellow pigment in the nervous layers, stretching over the whole central retina; i.e., the fovea, parafovea, and perifovea. The retina also contains the blind spot, which corresponds to the optic papilla (optic nerve head), the region on the nasal side of the retina through which the optic nerve fibres pass out of the eye.

Although the rods and cones may be said to form a mosaic, the retina is not organized in a simple mosaic fashion in the sense that each rod or cone is connected to a single bipolar cell that itself is connected to a single ganglion cell. There are only about 1,000,000 optic nerve fibres, while there are at least 150,000,000 receptors, so that there must be considerable convergence of receptors on the optic pathway. This means that there will be considerable mixing of messages. Furthermore, the retina contains additional nerve cells besides the bipolar and ganglion cells; these, the horizontal and amacrine cells, operate in the horizontal direction, allowing one area of the retina to influence the activity of another. In this way, for example, the messages from one part of the retina may be suppressed by a visual stimulus falling on another, an important element in the total of messages sent to the higher regions of the brain. Finally, it has been argued that some messages may be running the opposite way; they are called centrifugal and would allow one layer of the retina to affect another, or higher regions of the brain to control the responses of the retinal neurons. In primates the existence of these centrifugal fibres has been finally disproved, but in such lower vertebrates as the pigeon, their existence is quite certain.

Most of the optic nerve fibres in primates carry their messages to the lateral geniculate body, a relay station specifically concerned with vision. Some of the fibres separate from the main stream and run to a midbrain centre called the pretectal nucleus, which is a relay centre for pupillary responses to light.

Rods

Rod cells are photoreceptors that function as specialized neurons. They convert visual stimuli in the form of photons (particles of light) into chemical and electrical stimuli that can be processed by the central nervous system. Rod cells are stimulated by light over a wide range of intensities and are responsible for perceiving the size, shape, and brightness of visual images. They do not perceive colour and fine detail, tasks performed by the other major type of light-sensitive cell, the cone. Rod cells are much more sensitive to light than cones.

Rod cells have an elongated structure and consist of four distinct regions: an outer segment, an inner segment, the cell body, and the synaptic region. The outer segment contains the phototransduction apparatus. It is composed of a series of closely packed membrane disks that contain the photoreceptor molecule rhodopsin. Genetic mutations in the rhodopsin molecule have been shown to produce certain forms of retinitis pigmentosa, an inherited degenerative disease of the retinal pigments. The synaptic region is the site where the rod cell relays its information to intermediate neurons in the retina. These neurons connect with ganglion neurons whose axons form the approximately one million fibres of the optic nerve.

Rhodopsin is made up of a protein called opsin and a photosensitive chemical derived from vitamin A, 11-*cis*-retinaldehyde. Photons of light entering the eye cause the

11-*cis*-retinaldehyde to undergo isomerization (a change in configuration), forming all-*trans*-retinaldehyde. This isomerization activates the opsin protein, which then interacts with and activates a small protein called transducin. The association of opsin with transducin couples the external stimulus of light to an internal biochemical pathway that ultimately alters the release of neurotransmitters from the synaptic region of the cell. This changes the firing of the intermediate retinal neurons and affects the electrical impulses sent along the optic nerve to the brain. Such a complicated relay system allows for some integration and fine-tuning of these signals.

Rhodopsin molecules are broken down in sunlight or other bright viewing conditions. This breakdown prevents the overstimulation of the rod cells and makes them less sensitive to a bright environment. In dim light there is little breakdown of rhodopsin, and its persisting high concentration allows for better vision in a dark environment. Dark-adapted vision in humans is basically devoid of colour because it depends almost entirely on the functioning of rods.

Cones

Cones are the second type of photoreceptor occurring in the retina of the human eye. They are conical in shape and are associated with colour vision and perception of fine detail. Shorter and far fewer than the eye's rods, cones are less sensitive to low illumination levels and are mediators of photopic rather than scotopic (Greek *skotos,* "dark") vision. Cones are mostly concentrated within the central retina (macula), which contains the fovea (depression in the retina), where no rods are present. In contrast, the outer edges of the retina contain few cones and many rods. Chemical changes that occur when light strikes the cones are ultimately relayed as impulses to optic nerve fibres that enter the brain.

Macula Lutea

The macula lutea is the small yellowish area of the retina near the optic disk that provides central vision. When the gaze is fixed on any object, the centre of the macula, the centre of the lens, and the object are in a straight line. In the centre of the macula is the cone-containing fovea. Toward the centre of the macula there are no blood vessels to interfere with vision; thus, in this area of the retina, vision in bright light and colour perception are keenest.

Age-related macular degeneration (ARMD) is a relatively common condition in people over age 50. There are two forms of ARMD, known as wet and dry. In wet ARMD new blood vessels form beneath the retina that are very fragile and prone to breakage and bleeding, thereby compromising central vision acuity. As a result, wet ARMD advances more quickly and is more severe than dry ARMD, which is characterized by the presence of drusen (tiny yellow deposits on the retina) and the loss of retinal pigment and may progress so slowly that it goes unnoticed. Both conditions reduce central vision but do not interfere with peripheral vision.

Optic Disk

The optic disk (also known as the optic nerve head) is a small region within the retina in which there are no photoreceptors (i.e., rods or cones); thus there is no image detection in this area. The optic disk corresponds to the blind spot in the visual field of each eye. The blind spot of the right eye is located to the right of the centre of vision and vice versa in the left eye. With both eyes open, the blind spots are not perceived because the visual fields of the two eyes overlap. Indeed, even with one eye closed, the blind spot can be difficult to detect subjectively because of the ability of the brain to "fill in" or ignore the missing portion of the image.

The optic disk can be seen in the back of the eye with an ophthalmoscope. It is located on the nasal side of the macula lutea, is oval in shape, and is approximately 1.5 mm (0.06 inch) in diameter. It is also the entry point into the eye for major blood vessels that serve the retina. The optic disk represents the beginning of the optic nerve (second cranial nerve) and the point where axons from over one million retinal ganglion cells coalesce. Clinical evaluation of the optic nerve head is critical in the diagnosis and monitoring of glaucoma and other optic neuropathies that may lead to vision loss.

Optic Nerve

The optic nerve is the second cranial nerve, which carries sensory nerve impulses from the more than one million ganglion cells of the retina toward the visual centres in the brain. The vast majority of optic nerve fibres convey information regarding central vision.

The optic nerve begins at the optic disk at the back of the eye. The optic disk forms from the convergence of ganglion cell output fibres (called axons) as they pass out of the eye. When the nerve emerges from the back of the eye, it passes through the remainder of the posterior orbit (eye socket) and through the bony optic canal to emerge intracranially on the underside of the front of the brain. At this point the optic nerve from each eye comes together and forms an X-shaped structure called the optic chiasm. Here, approximately one-half of the nerve fibres from each eye continue on the same side of the brain, and the remaining nerve fibres cross over at the chiasm to join fibres from the opposite eye on the other side of the brain. This arrangement is essential for producing binocular vision. Posterior to the optic chiasm, the nerve fibres travel in optic tracts to various portions of the brain—predominantly the lateral geniculate nuclei. Fibres from the lateral geniculate nuclei form the optic radiations that course toward the visual cortex located in the occipital lobes in the back of the brain. Some nerve fibres leave the optic tract without entering the lateral geniculate nuclei and instead enter the brain stem to provide information that ultimately determines pupil size.

The retina, optic disk, optic nerve, optic chiasm, optic tracts, optic radiations, and visual centres of the brain are topographically organized to correspond to particular areas of the visual field. Therefore, damage to, or pressure on, particular portions of these structures can produce characteristic deficits in a person's visual field. The affected person may or may not notice these visual field defects.

TRANSPARENT MEDIA OF THE EYE

Within the cavities enclosed by the three layers of the eyeball there are the aqueous humour in the anterior and posterior chambers; the crystalline lens behind the iris; and the vitreous body, which fills the large cavity behind the lens and iris.

THE AQUEOUS HUMOUR

The aqueous humour is an optically clear, slightly alkaline liquid that occupies the anterior and posterior chambers of the eye. The aqueous humour resembles blood plasma in composition but contains less protein and glucose and more lactic acid and ascorbic acid. It provides these nutrients (as well as oxygen) to eye tissues that lack a direct blood supply (such as the lens) and also removes their waste products. In addition, it provides an internal pressure, known as intraocular pressure, that keeps the eyeball (globe) properly formed. Aqueous humour is formed from the blood by filtration, secretion, and diffusion through the ciliary body, a muscular structure located behind the iris that controls the curvature of the lens.

Aqueous humour leaves the eye through the porous trabecular meshwork and flows into Schlemm's canal, a ringlike passageway around the outer angle of the anterior chamber in front of the iris. The canal of Schlemm encircles the cornea and connects by small connector channels to the blood vessels buried in the sclera and forming the intrascleral plexus or network. From this plexus the blood, containing the aqueous humour, passes into more superficial vessels; it finally leaves the eye in the anterior ciliary veins. The wall of the canal that faces the aqueous humour is very delicate and allows the fluid to percolate through by virtue of the relatively high pressure of the fluid within the eye. Obstruction of this exit, for example, if the iris is pushed forward to cover the wall of the canal, causes a sharp rise in the pressure within the eye, a condition that is known as glaucoma. Often the obstruction is not obvious, but is caused perhaps by a hardening of the tissue just adjacent to the wall of the canal—the trabecular meshwork, in which case the rise of pressure is more gradual and insidious. Ultimately the abnormal pressure damages the retina and causes a variable degree of blindness.

Therapies for glaucoma are aimed at lowering eye pressure by increasing the outflow of aqueous humour from the eye and decreasing its production by the ciliary body. Two types of surgery that increase outflow of fluid from the eye include trabeculoplasty, a type of laser surgery that increases the permeability of the trabecular meshwork, and trabeculectomy (also called filtering microsurgery). Trabeculectomy diverts aqueous humour from the anterior chamber inside the eye to the space under the conjunctiva (the transparent skin that covers the sclera).

The normal intraocular pressure is about 15 mm (0.6 inch) of mercury above atmospheric pressure, so that if the anterior chamber is punctured by a hypodermic needle the aqueous humour flows out readily. Its function in maintaining the eye reasonably hard is seen by the collapse and wrinkling of the cornea when the fluid is allowed to escape. An additional function of the fluid is to provide nutrition for the crystalline lens and also for the cornea, both of which are devoid of blood vessels; the steady renewal and drainage serve to bring into the eye various nutrient substances, including glucose and amino acids, and to remove waste products of metabolism.

VITREOUS BODY

The vitreous body is a semisolid gel structure that is remarkable for the small amount of solid matter that it contains. The solid material is made up of a form of collagen, vitrosin, and hyaluronic acid (a mucopolysaccharide). Thus, its composition is rather similar to that of the cornea, but the proportion of water is much greater, about 98 percent or more, compared with about 75 percent for the cornea. The jelly is probably secreted by certain cells of the retina. In general, the vitreous body is devoid of cells, in contrast with the lens, which is packed tight with cells. Embedded in the surface of the vitreous body, however, there is a population of specialized cells, the hyalocytes of Balazs, which may contribute to the breakdown and renewal of the hyaluronic acid. The vitreous body serves to keep the underlying retina pressed against the choroid.

CRYSTALLINE LENS

The lens is a transparent body, flatter on its anterior (front) than on its posterior (rear) surface, and suspended within the eye by the zonular fibres of Zinn attached to its equator; its anterior surface is bathed by aqueous humour, and its posterior surface by the vitreous body. The lens is a mass of tightly packed transparent fibrous cells, the lens fibres, enclosed in an elastic collagenous capsule. The lens fibres are arranged in sheets that form successive layers; the fibres run from pole to pole of the lens, the middle of a given fibre being in the equatorial region. On meridional (horizontal) section, the fibres are cut longitudinally to give an onion-scale appearance, whereas a section at right-angles to this—an equatorial section—would cut all the fibres across, and the result would be to give a honeycomb appearance. The epithelium, covering the anterior surface of the lens under the capsule, serves as the origin of the lens fibres, both during embryonic and fetal development and during infant and adult life, the lens continuing to grow by the laying down of new fibres throughout life.

SUPPORTING STRUCTURES

ORBIT

The eye is protected from mechanical injury by being enclosed in a socket, or orbit, which is made up of portions of several of the bones of the skull to form a four-sided pyramid the apex of which points back into the head. Thus, the floor of the orbit is made up of parts of the maxilla, zygomatic, and palatine bones, while the roof is made up of the orbital plate of the frontal bone and, behind this, by the lesser wing of the sphenoid. The optic foramen, the opening through which the optic nerve runs back into the brain and the large ophthalmic artery enters the orbit, is at the nasal side of the apex; the superior orbital fissure is a larger hole through which pass large veins and nerves. These nerves may carry nonvisual sensory messages—e.g., pain—or they may be motor nerves controlling the muscles of the eye. There are other fissures and canals transmitting nerves and blood vessels. The eyeball and its functional muscles are surrounded by a layer of orbital fat that acts much like a cushion, permitting a smooth rotation of the eyeball about a virtually fixed point, the centre of rotation. The protrusion of the eyeballs—proptosis—in exophthalmic goitre is caused by the collection of fluid in the orbital fatty tissue.

EYELIDS

It is vitally important that the front surface of the eyeball, the cornea, remain moist. This is achieved by the eyelids, which during waking hours sweep the secretions of the lacrimal apparatus and other glands over the surface at regular intervals and which during sleep cover the eyes and prevent evaporation. Maintaining moisture levels is vital for the normal functioning of the conjunctiva and cornea. The conjunctiva is the mucous membrane that lines the eyelid and covers the visible portion of the eyeball except the cornea.

The lids are essentially folds of tissue covering the front of the orbit and, when the eye is open, leaving an almond-shaped aperture. The points of the almond are called canthi; that nearest the nose is the inner canthus, and the other is the outer canthus. The lid may be divided into four layers: (1) the skin, containing glands that open onto the surface of the lid margin, and the eyelashes; (2) a muscular layer containing principally the orbicularis oculi muscle, responsible for lid closure; (3) a fibrous layer that gives the lid its mechanical stability, its principal portions being the tarsal plates, which border directly upon the opening between the lids, called the palpebral aperture; and (4) the innermost layer of the lid, a portion of the con- junctiva. The conjunctiva is a mucous membrane that serves to attach the eyeball to the orbit and lids but per- mits a considerable degree of rotation of the eyeball in the orbit. The lid borders are kept lubricated by an oily secre- tion (called sebum) of the meibomian glands. This secretion forms part of the tear film and reduces evapora- tive tear loss.

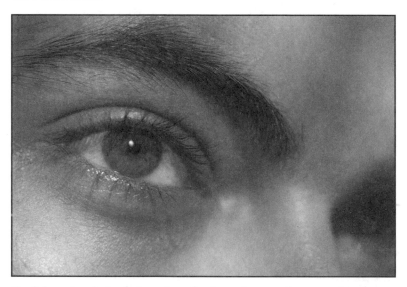

Eyelids and eyelashes help to keep foreign substances from entering the eye. Shutterstock.com

The movable tissues of the eyelids, namely the skin and muscle, enable them to help prevent injuries to the eye from foreign bodies. The primary defense provided by the eyelids is the blink reflex. Impulses for eyelid closing come by way of the facial (seventh cranial) nerve, and for opening by way of the oculomotor (third cranial) nerve.

Conjunctiva

The conjunctiva lines the eyelids and then bends back over the surface of the eyeball, constituting an outer covering to the forward part of this and terminating at the transparent region of the eye, the cornea. The portion that lines the lids is called the palpebral portion of the conjunctiva; the portion covering the white of the eyeball is called the bulbar conjunctiva. Between the bulbar and the palpebral conjunctiva there are two loose, redundant portions forming recesses that project back toward the equator of the globe. These recesses are called the upper and lower fornices, or conjunctival sacs; it is the looseness of the conjunctiva at these points that makes movements of lids and eyeball possible.

Fibrous Layer

The fibrous layer, which gives the lid its mechanical stability, is made up of the thick, and relatively rigid, tarsal plates, bordering directly on the palpebral aperture, and the much thinner palpebral fascia, or sheet of connective tissue; the two together are called the septum orbitale. When the lids are closed, the whole opening of the orbit is covered by this septum. Two ligaments, the medial and lateral palpebral ligaments, attached to the orbit and to the septum orbitale, stabilize the position of the lids in relation to the globe. The medial ligament is by far the stronger.

Muscles of the Lids

Closure of the lids is achieved by contraction of the orbicularis muscle, a single oval sheet of muscle extending from the regions of the forehead and face and surrounding the orbit into the lids. It is divided into orbital and palpebral portions, and it is essentially the palpebral portion, within the lid, that causes lid closure. The palpebral portion passes across the lids from a ligament called the medial palpebral ligament and from the neighbouring bone of the orbit in a series of half ellipses that meet outside the outer corner of the eye, the lateral canthus, to form a band of fibres called the lateral palpebral raphe. Additional parts of the orbicularis have been given separate names—namely, Horner's muscle and the muscle of Riolan; they come into close relation with the lacrimal apparatus and assist in drainage of the tears. The muscle of Riolan, lying close to the lid margins, contributes to keeping the lids in close apposition. The orbital portion of the orbicularis is not normally concerned with blinking, which may be carried out entirely by the palpebral portion; however, it is concerned with closing the eyes tightly. The skin of the forehead, temple, and cheek is then drawn toward the medial (nose) side of the orbit, and the radiating furrows, formed by this action of the orbital portion, eventually lead to the so-called crow's feet of elderly persons. It must be appreciated that the two portions can be activated independently; thus, the orbital portion may contract, causing a furrowing of the brows that reduces the amount of light entering from above, while the palpebral portion remains relaxed and allows the eyes to remain open.

Opening of the eye is not just the result of passive relaxation of the orbicularis muscle but also is the effect of the contraction of the levator palpebrae superioris muscle of the upper lid. This muscle takes origin with the extraocular muscles at the apex of the orbit as a narrow tendon and runs forward into the upper lid as a broad tendon, the levator aponeurosis, which is attached to the forward surface of the tarsus and the skin covering the upper lid. Contraction of the muscle causes elevation of the upper eyelid. The nervous connections of this muscle are closely related to those of the extraocular muscle required to elevate the eye, so that when the eye looks upward the upper eyelid tends to move up in unison.

The orbicularis and levator are striated muscles under voluntary control. The eyelids also contain smooth (involuntary) muscle fibres that are activated by the sympathetic division of the autonomic system and tend to widen the palpebral fissure (the eye opening) by elevation of the upper, and depression of the lower, lid.

In addition to the muscles already described, other facial muscles often cooperate in the act of lid closure or opening. Thus, the corrugator supercilii muscles pull the eyebrows toward the bridge of the nose, making a projecting "roof" over the medial angle of the eye and producing characteristic furrows in the forehead; the roof is used primarily to protect the eye from the glare of the sun. The pyramidalis, or procerus, muscles occupy the bridge of the nose; they arise from the lower portion of the nasal bones and are attached to the skin of the lower part of the forehead on either side of the midline; they pull the skin into transverse furrows. In lid opening, the frontalis muscle, arising high on the forehead, midway between the coronal suture, a seam across the top of the skull, and the orbital margin, is attached to the skin of the eyebrows. Contraction therefore causes the eyebrows to rise and opposes the action of the orbital portion of the orbicularis; the muscle is especially used when one gazes upward. It is also brought into action when vision is rendered difficult either by distance or the absence of sufficient light.

Skin

The outermost layer of the eyelid is the skin, with features not greatly different from skin on the rest of the body, with the possible exception of large pigment cells, which, although found elsewhere, are much more numerous in the skin of the lids. The cells may wander, and it is these movements of the pigment cells that determine the changes in colouration seen in some people with alterations in health. The skin has sweat glands and hairs. As the junction between skin and conjunctiva is approached, the hairs change their character to become eyelashes.

TEAR DUCTS AND GLANDS

Tear ducts and glands, also called lacrimal ducts and glands, are structures that produce and distribute the watery component of the tear film. Tears are constantly secreted at a relatively regular rate from satellite (or accessory) lacrimal glands located high in the superior upper lid. Reflex tearing, such as that stimulated by eye irritation, bright lights, or emotional upset, is provided by the main lacrimal glands. Each main lacrimal gland lies in a hollow space in the inner surfaces of the frontal bone, located above and laterally to the eye. Each is about the size and shape of a shelled almond and is divided by a fibrous partition into an upper and a lower portion. Ducts from the gland discharge the tears onto the eye surface through openings, where the conjunctiva lining the upper lid meets the conjunctiva that covers the eyeball (an area called the fornix). Tears leave each eye by way of upper and lower canalicular ducts, which have barely visible openings, called puncta, at the nasal end of the upper and lower lid margins. The canaliculi lead to the lacrimal sac near the inner corner of each eye, which itself empties into the nasolacrimal duct, a tubelike structure that directs tears into the nasal cavity.

Tears consist of a complex and usually clear fluid that is diffused between the eye and the eyelid. Further components of the tear film include an inner mucous layer produced by specialized conjunctival cells and an outer lipid layer produced by meibomian, or tarsal, glands, which consist of a row of elongated glands extending through the tarsal plates along the eyelid margin. The meibomian glands secrete an oil that emerges onto the surface of the lid margin and acts as a barrier for the tear fluid, which accumulates in the grooves between the eyeball and the lid barriers. Thus, the mucous layer helps the tear film adhere to the eye surface, while the lipid layer serves to reduce tear evaporation. Tears prevent excessive drying of the surfaces of the eye (such as the conjunctiva and cornea), provide some nutrition and oxygen to surface structures, and possess antibacterial properties.

Diseases that damage the lacrimal gland, and thus decrease tear secretion, can lead to chronic dry eye, which ultimately can threaten vision. Treatment of chronic dry eye consists of artificial lubrication and, in some cases, mechanical closure of the puncta or surgery to partially close the lids.

EXTRAOCULAR MUSCLES

Six muscles outside the eye govern its movements. These muscles are the four rectus muscles—the inferior, medial, lateral, and superior recti—and the superior and inferior oblique muscles. The rectus muscles arise from a fibrous ring that encircles the optic nerve at the optic foramen, the opening through which the nerve passes, and are attached to the sclera, the opaque portion of the eyeball, in front of the equator, or widest part, of the eye. The superior oblique muscle arises near the rim of the optic foramen and somewhat nearer the nose than the origin of the rectus medialis. It ends in a rounded tendon that passes through a fibrous ring, the trochlea, that is attached to the frontal bone. The trochlea acts as a pulley. The tendon is attached to the sclera back of the equator of the eye.

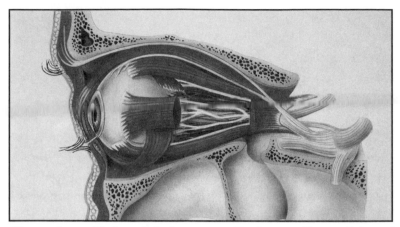

The muscles outside the eye help them to move. De Agostini Picture Library/ Getty Images

The inferior oblique muscle originates from the floor of the orbit, passes under the eyeball like a sling, and is attached to the sclera between the attachments of the superior and lateral rectus muscles. The rectus muscles direct the gaze upward and downward and from side to side. The inferior oblique muscle tends to direct the eye upward, and the superior oblique to depress the eye; because of the obliqueness of the pull, each causes the eye to roll, and in an opposite direction.

The oblique muscles are strictly antagonistic to each other, but they work with the vertical rectus muscles in so far as the superior rectus and inferior oblique both tend to elevate the gaze and the inferior rectus and superior oblique both tend to depress the gaze. The superior and inferior recti do not produce a pure action of elevation or depression because their plane of action is not exactly vertical; in consequence, as with the obliques, they cause some degree of rolling (torsion), but by no means so great as that caused by the obliques; the direction of rolling caused by the rectus muscle is opposite to that of its synergistic oblique; the superior rectus causes the eye to roll inward, and the inferior oblique outward.

CHAPTER 2
PROTECTION AND MOVEMENTS OF THE EYE

The protection of the eye from physical injury is crucial in a world where damage to the visual apparatus is under threat from environmental factors, such as wind and heat, and from myriad other harmful elements, including infectious organisms and chemicals. Various structures of the eye play fundamental roles in protection, with the first line of defense being the eyelids.

Movements of the eye are important for controlling and optimizing vision. Small muscles attached to the eye function to change the shape of the lens, as well as the shape of the eyeball itself, enabling vision to be focused on objects at varying distances. In addition, guided by finely controlled muscles, the human eye can rotate independently of head movement. Such ability to move the eyes without moving the head or body is useful for viewing objects that occur in the periphery of the visual field and is especially important if the neck or body becomes immobilized due to paralysis.

PROTECTIVE MECHANISMS

The first line of protection of the eyes is provided by the eyelids, which prevent access of foreign bodies and assist in the lubrication of the corneal surface. Lid closure and opening are accomplished by the orbicularis oculi and levator palpebri muscles; the orbicularis oculi operates on both lids, bringing their margins into close apposition in the act of lid closure. Opening results from relaxation of the orbicularis muscle and contraction of the levator palpebri of the upper lid; the smooth muscle of the upper lid, Müller's muscle, or the superior palpebral muscle, also assists in widening the lid aperture.

The lower eyelid does not possess a muscle corresponding to the levator (a muscle that raises a body part) of the upper lid, and the only muscle available for causing an active lowering of the lid, required during the depression of the gaze, is the inferior palpebral muscle, which is analogous to the muscle of Müller of the upper lid (called the superior palpebral muscle). This inferior palpebral muscle is so directly fused with the sheaths of the ocular muscles that it provides cooperative action, opening of the lid on downward gaze being mediated, in effect, mainly by the inferior rectus.

INNERVATION

The seventh cranial nerve — the facial nerve — supplies the motor fibres for the orbicularis muscle. The levator, is innervated, or stimulated into action, by the third cranial nerve — the oculomotor nerve. This nerve also innervates some of the extraocular muscles concerned with rotation of the eyeball, including the superior rectus. The smooth muscle of the eyelids and orbit is activated by the sympathetic division of the autonomic system. The secretion of adrenaline during such states of excitement as fear would also presumably cause contraction of the smooth muscle, but it seems unlikely that this would lead to the protrusion of the eyes traditionally associated with extreme fear. It is possible that the widening of the lid aperture occurring in this excited state, and dilation of the pupil, create the illusion of eye protrusion.

Blinking is normally an involuntary act but may be carried out voluntarily. The more vigorous "full closure" of the lids involves the orbital portion of the orbicularis muscle and may be accompanied by contraction of the facial muscles that have been described as accessory muscles of blinking: namely, the corrugator supercilii, which on contraction pulls the eyebrows toward the bridge of the nose; and the procerus or pyramidalis, which pulls the skin of the forehead into horizontal folds, acting as a protection when the eyes are exposed to bright light. The more vigorous full closure may be evoked as a reflex response.

BLINK REFLEXES

Reflex blinking may be caused by practically any peripheral stimulus, but the two functionally significant reflexes are (1) that resulting from stimulation of the endings of the fifth cranial nerve in the cornea, lid, or conjunctiva—the sensory blink reflex, or corneal reflex—and (2) that caused by bright light—the optical blink reflex. The corneal reflex is rapid (0.1 second reflex time) and is the last to disappear in deepening anesthesia, impulses being relayed from the nucleus of the fifth nerve to the seventh cranial nerve, which transmits the motor impulses. The reflex is said to be under the control of a medullary centre. The optical reflex is slower; in humans, the nervous pathway includes the visual cortex (the outer substance of the brain; the visual centre is located in the occipital—rear—lobe). The reflex is absent in children of less than nine months.

In the waking hours the eyes blink fairly regularly at intervals of two to 10 seconds, the actual rate being a characteristic of the individual. The function of this is to spread the lacrimal secretions over the cornea. It might be thought that each blink would be reflexly determined by a corneal stimulus—drying and irritation—but extensive studies indicate that this view is wrong; the normal blinking rate is apparently determined by the activity of a "blinking centre" in the globus pallidus of the caudate nucleus, a mass of nerve cells between the base and the outer substance of the brain. This is not to deny that the blink rate is modified by external stimuli.

There is a strong association between blinking and the action of the extraocular muscles. Eye movement is generally accompanied by a blink, and it is thought that this aids the eyes in changing their fixation point.

SECRETION OF TEARS

The exposed surface of the globe (eyeball) is kept moist by the tears secreted by the lacrimal apparatus, together with the mucous and oily secretions of the other secretory organs and cells of the lids and conjunctiva. The secretion produces what has been called the precorneal film, which consists of an inner layer of mucus, a middle layer of lacrimal secretion, and an outer oily film that reduces the rate of evaporation of the underlying watery layer. The normal daily (24-hour) rate of secretion has been estimated at about 0.75 to 1.1 grams (0.03 to 0.04 ounce); secretion tends to decrease with age. Chemical analysis of the tears reveals a typical body fluid with a salt concentration similar to that of blood plasma. An interesting component is lysozyme, an enzyme that has bactericidal action by virtue of its power of dissolving away the outer coats of many bacteria.

Tears are secreted reflexly in response to a variety of stimuli—e.g., irritative stimuli to the cornea, conjunctiva, nasal mucosa; hot or peppery stimuli applied to the mouth and tongue; or bright lights. In addition, tear flow occurs in association with vomiting, coughing, and yawning. The secretion associated with emotional upset is called psychical weeping. Severing of the sensory root of the trigeminal (fifth cranial) nerve prevents all reflex weeping, leaving psychical weeping unaffected; similarly, the application of cocaine to the surface of the eye, which paralyzes the sensory nerve endings, inhibits reflex weeping, even when the eye is exposed to potent tear gases. The afferent (sensory) pathway in the reflex is thus by way of the fifth cranial, or the trigeminal nerve. The motor innervation is by way of the autonomic (involuntary) division; the parasympathetic supply derived from the facial nerve (the seventh cranial nerve) seems to have the dominant motor influence. Thus, drugs that mimic the parasympathetic input, such as acetylcholine, provoke secretion, and secretion may be blocked by such typical anticholinergic drugs as atropine.

Psychical weeping is weeping caused by emotion. Shutterstock.com

Innervation of the lacrimal gland is not always complete at birth, so the newborn infant is generally said to cry without weeping. Because absence of reflex tearing fails to produce any serious drying of the cornea, and surgical destruction of the main lacrimal gland is often without serious consequences, it seems likely that the subsidiary secretion from the accessory lacrimal glands is adequate to keep the cornea moist. The reflex secretion that produces abundant tears may be regarded as an emergency response.

A drainage mechanism for tears is necessary only during copious secretion. The mechanism, described as the lacrimal pump, consists of alternately negative and positive pressure in the lacrimal sac caused by the contraction of the orbicularis muscle during blinking.

MOVEMENTS OF THE EYES

Because only a small portion of the retina, the fovea, is actually employed for distinct vision, it is vitally important that the motor apparatus governing the direction of gaze be extremely precise in its operation, and rapid. Thus, the gaze must shift swiftly and accurately during the process of reading. Again, if the gaze must remain fixed on a single small object—e.g., a golf ball—the eyes must keep adjusting their gaze to compensate for the continuous small movements of the head and to maintain the image exactly on the fovea. The extraocular muscles that carry out these movements are under voluntary control; thus, the direction of regard can be changed deliberately. Most of the actual movements of the eyes are carried out without awareness, however, in response to movements of the objects in the environment, or in response to movements of the head or the rest of the body, and so on. In examining the mechanisms of the eye movements, then, one must resolve them into a number of reflex responses to changes in the environment or the individual, remembering, of course, that there is an overriding voluntary control.

AXES OF THE EYE

It is worthwhile at this point to define certain axes of the eyes employed during different types of study. The optic axis of the eye is a line drawn through the centre of the cornea and the nodal (central) point of the eye; it actually does not intersect with the retina at the centre of the fovea as might be expected, but toward the nose from this, so that there is an angle of about five degrees between (1) the visual axis—the line joining the point fixated (the point toward which the gaze is directed) and the nodal point—and (2) the optic axis.

ACTIONS OF THE MUSCLES

The general modes of action of the six extraocular muscles can be described in connection with their anatomy: rotation of the eye toward the nose is carried out by the medial rectus; outward movement is by the lateral rectus. Upward movements are carried out by the combined actions of the superior rectus and the inferior oblique muscles, and downward movements by the inferior rectus and the superior oblique. Intermediate directions of gaze are achieved by combined actions of several muscles. When the two eyes act together, as they normally do, and change their direction of gaze to the left, for example, the left eye rotates away from the nose by means of its lateral rectus, while the right eye turns toward the nose by means of its medial rectus. These muscles may be considered as a linked pair; that is, when they are activated by the central nervous system this occurs conjointly and virtually automatically. This linking of the muscles of the two eyes is an important physiological feature and has still more important pathological interest in the analysis of squint, when the two eyes fail to be directed at the same point.

BINOCULAR MOVEMENTS

The binocular movements (the movements of the two eyes) fall into two classes, the conjugate movements, when both eyes move in the same direction, as in a change in the direction of gaze, and disjunctive movements, when the eyes move in opposite directions. Thus, during convergence onto a near object both eyes move toward the nose; the movement is horizontal, but disjunctive, by contrast with the conjugate movement when both eyes move, say, to the right. The disjunctive movement of convergence can be carried out voluntarily, but the act is usually brought about reflexly in response to the changed optical situation—i.e., the nearness of the object of gaze. A seesaw movement of the eyes, whereby one eye looks upward and the other downward, is possible, but not voluntarily; to achieve this a prism is placed in front on one eye so that the object seen through it appears displaced upward or downward; the other eye sees the object where it is. The result of such an arrangement is that, unless the eye with the prism in front makes an upward or downward movement, independent of the other, the images will not fall on corresponding parts of the retinas in the two eyes. Such a noncorrespondence of the retinal images causes double vision; to avoid this, there is an adjustment in the alignment of the eyes so that a seesaw movement is actually executed.

In a similar way, the eyes may be made to undergo torsion, or rolling. A conjugate torsion, in which both eyes rotate about their anteroposterior (fore-and-aft) axes in

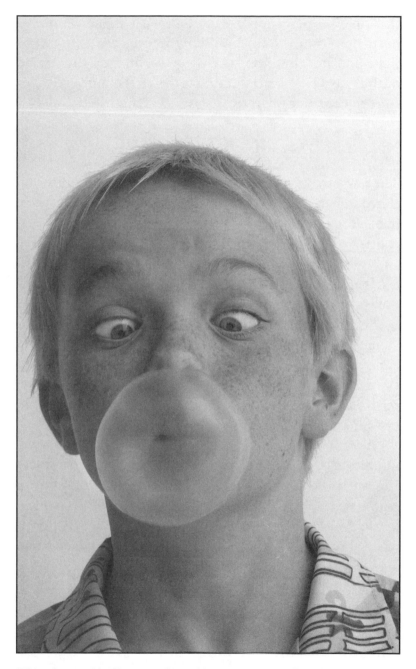

This photograph illustrates disjunctive movement, when the eyes move in opposite directions. Thus, during convergence onto a near object both eyes move toward the nose. Tancrediphoto.com/Iconica/Getty Images

the same sense, occurs naturally; for example, when the head tips toward one shoulder the eyes tend to roll in the opposite direction, with the result that the image of the visual field on the retina tends to remain vertical in spite of the rotation of the head.

NERVOUS CONTROL

The nerves controlling the actions of the muscles are the third, fourth, and sixth cranial nerves, with their bodies (nuclei) in the brainstem; the third, or oculomotor nerve, controls the superior and inferior recti, the medial rectus, and inferior oblique; the fourth cranial nerve, the trochlear nerve, controls the superior oblique; and the sixth, the abducens nerve, controls the lateral rectus. The nuclei of these nerves are closely associated; especially, there are connections between the nuclei of the sixth cranial nerve, controlling the lateral rectus, and the nucleus of the third, controlling the medial rectus; it is through this close relationship that the linking of the lateral rectus of one eye and the medial rectus of the other is achieved.

Another type of linking is concerned with reciprocal inhibition; that is, when there are two antagonistic muscles, such as the medial and the lateral rectus, contraction of one is accompanied by a simultaneous inhibition of the other. Muscles show a continuous slight activity even when at rest; this keeps them taut; this action, called tonic activity, is brought about by discharges in the motor nerve to the muscle. Hence, when the agonist muscle contracts its antagonist must be inhibited.

REFLEX PATHWAYS

In examining any reflex movement one must look for the sensory input—i.e., the way in which messages in sensory nerves bring about discharges in the motor nerves to the muscles; this study involves the connections of the motor nerves or nuclei with other centres of the brain.

When a subject is looking straight ahead and a bright light appears in the periphery of the field of vision, the subject's eyes automatically turn to fix on the light; this is called the fixation reflex. The sensory pathway in the reflex arc leads as far as the cerebral cortex because removal of the occipital cortex (the outer brain substance at the back of the head) abolishes reflex eye movements in response to light stimuli. If the occipital cortex is stimulated electrically, movements of the eyes may be induced, and in fact one may draw a pattern of the visual field on the occipital cortex corresponding with the directions in which the gaze is turned when given points on the cortex are stimulated. This pattern corresponds with the pattern obtained by recording the visual responses to light stimuli from different parts of the visual field. The remainder of the pathway—i.e., from the occipital cortex to the motor neurons in the brainstem—has long been considered to involve the superior colliculi, a paired formation on the roof of the midbrain, as relay stations, and they certainly have such a role in lower animals; but in humans a pathway from the cortex to the eye-muscle nuclei independent of the superior colliculi of the midbrain is generally assumed.

Continual movements of the eyes occur even when an effort is made to maintain steady fixation of an object. Some of these movements may be regarded as manifestations of the fixation reflex; thus, the eyes tend to drift off their target, and, because of this, the fixation reflex comes into play, bringing the eyes back on target. Experimentally, the fixation reflex can be studied by observation of the regular to-and-fro movements of the eyes as they follow a rotating drum striped in black and white. (Such movements of the eyes directed at a moving object are called optokinetic nystagmus; nystagmus itself is the involuntary movement of the eye back and forth, up and down, or in a rotatory or a mixed fashion.) While the eyes watch the moving drum, they involuntarily make a slow movement as a result of fixing their gaze on a particular stripe. At a certain point, fixation is broken off, and the eyes spring back to fix on a new stripe. Thus, the nystagmus consists of a slow movement with angular velocity equal to that of the rotation of the drum, then a fast saccade, or jump from one point of fixation to another, in the opposite direction; the process is repeated indefinitely.

Another type of nystagmus reveals the play of another set of reflexes. These are mediated by the semicircular canals—i.e., the organs of balance or the vestibular apparatus. Such a reflex may be evoked by rotating the subject in a chair at a steady speed; the eyes move slowly in the opposite direction to that of rotation and, at the end of their excursion, jump back with a fast saccade in the direction of rotation. If rotation suddenly ceases, the eyes go into a nystagmus in the opposite direction, the postrotatory nystagmus.

During rotation, certain semicircular canals are being stimulated, and the important point is that any acceleration of the head that stimulates these canals will cause reflex movements of the eyes; thus, acceleration of the head to the right causes a movement of the eyes to the left, the function of the reflex being to enable the eyes to maintain steady fixation of an object despite movements of the head. The reflex occurs even when the eyes are shut, and, when the eyes are open, it obviously cooperates with the fixation reflex in maintaining steady fixation. In many lower animals this connection between organs of balance and eyes is very rigid; thus, one may move the tail of a fish, and its eyes will move reflexly. In humans, in addition to the semicircular canals, the gravity organ—the utricle—and the stretch receptors in the muscles of the neck also function in close relation to the eye muscles. Thus, when the head is turned upward, there is a reflex tendency for the eyes to move downward, even if the eyes are shut. The actual movement is probably initiated by the reflex from the semicircular canals, which respond to acceleration, but the maintenance of the position is brought about by a reflex through the stretch of the neck muscles and also through the pull of gravity on the utricle, or otolith organ, in the inner ear.

Voluntary Centre

The eyes are under voluntary control, and it is thought that the cortical area subserving voluntary eye movements is in the frontal cortex. Stimulation of this in primates causes movements of the eyes that are well coordinated, and a movement induced by this region prevails over one induced by stimulation of the occipital cortex. The existence of a separate centre in humans is revealed by certain neurological disorders in which the subject is unable to fixate voluntarily but can do so reflexly.

Nature of Eye Movements

By the use of refined methods of measuring the position of the eyes at any moment, it becomes immediately evident that the eyes are never stationary for more than a fraction of a second; the movements are of three types: (1) irregular movements of high frequency (30–70 per second) and small excursions of about 20 seconds of arc; (2) flicks, or saccades, of several minutes of arc occurring at regular intervals of about one second; and between these saccades there occur (3) slow irregular drifts extending up to six minutes of arc. The saccades are corrective, serving to bring the fixation axis on the point of regard after this has drifted away from it too far, and thus are a manifestation of the fixation reflex.

The significance of these small movements during fixation was revealed by studies on the stabilized retinal image. By a suitable optical device the image of an object could be held stationary on the retina in spite of the movements of the eye. It was found that under these conditions the image would disappear within a few seconds. Thus, the movements of the eye are apparently necessary to allow the contours of the image to fall on a new set of rods and cones at repeated intervals; if this does not occur, the retina adapts to their stimulus and ceases to send messages to the central nervous system.

Small flicks are essentially the same as the larger movement made when the two eyes fixate (fix on) a light when it suddenly appears in the peripheral field; this is given the general name of saccade, to distinguish it from the slower movements occurring during convergence and smooth following. Saccades may involve the eyes alone or, more commonly, the eyes and the head. Their function is to place the fovea, the central region of the retina where vision is most acute, onto the images of parts of the visual scene of interest. Their duration and peak velocity vary systematically with their size. The smallest "microsaccades" move the eye through only a few minutes of arc (one minute of arc equals one-sixtieth of one degree). They last about 20 milliseconds and have maximum velocities of about 10° per second. The largest saccades (excluding the contributions of head movements) can be up to 100°, with a duration of up to 300 milliseconds and a maximum velocity of about 500–700° per second.

During saccades, vision is seriously impaired for two reasons. First, during large saccades, the image is moving so fast that it is blurred and unusable. Second, an active blanking-off process, known as saccadic suppression, occurs, and this blocks vision for the first part of each saccade. Between saccades, the eyes are held stationary in fixations. It is during these periods, which last on average about 190 milliseconds, that the eyes take in visual information. Saccades can be reflexive in nature; for example, when an object appears in one's peripheral field of view. However, as Russian psychologist Alfred L. Yarbus showed, saccades are often information-seeking in nature, directed to particular objects or regions by the requirements of ongoing behaviour.

A remarkable feature of saccades is the apparent absence of significant inertia in the eyeball, so that movement is halted, not by any checking action of antagonistic muscles but simply by cessation of contraction of the agonists. Once under way, the saccade is determined in amount, so that the subject cannot voluntarily alter its direction and extent. The control mechanism for the saccadic type of movement can be described as a sampled data system, i.e., the brain makes discontinuous samples of the position of the eyes in relation to the target and corrects the error, in contrast to a continuous feedback system that takes account of the error all the time.

The movements of the eyes when they converge onto a near object are in remarkable contrast to the saccade; the angular velocity is only about 25° per second, compared with values as high as 700° per second in the saccade. The great difference in speed between the two movements is believed to be the result of their being under the control of different muscle fibres. The extraocular muscles contain two types of muscle fibre, slow and fast, which are innervated by different nerve supplies. Because these nerves control different types of muscle movement, they enable the extraocular muscle to twitch rapidly or to contract slowly.

If a moving light suddenly appears in the field of view, and if its rate of movement is less than about 30° per second, the response of the eyes is remarkably efficient; a saccade brings the eyes on target, and they follow the motion at almost exactly the same angular velocity as that of the target; inaccuracies in following lead to corrective saccades. When the rate of movement of the target is greater than about 30° per second, these corrective saccades become more obvious because now smooth following is not possible; the eyes make constant-velocity movements, but the velocity rarely matches that of the moving target, so that there must be frequent corrective saccades. Studies have shown that the following movements are highly integrated and must involve a continuous feedback system whereby errors are used to modify the performance. Thus, the systems for control of saccades and tracking movements are fundamentally different.

WORK OF THE LENS SYSTEM

REFRACTION

The optical system of the eye is such as to produce a reduced inverted image of the visual field on the retina; the system behaves as a convex lens but is, in fact, much more complex, refraction taking place not at two surfaces, as in a lens, but at four separate surfaces—at the anterior and the posterior surfaces of the cornea and of the crystalline lens. Each of these surfaces is approximately spherical, and at each optical interface—e.g., between air and the anterior surface of the cornea—the bending of a ray of light is toward the axis, so that, in effect, there are four surfaces tending to make rays of light converge on each other. If the rays of light falling on the cornea are parallel—i.e., if they come from a distant point—the net effect of this series of refractions at the four surfaces is to bring these rays to a point, enabling the optical system to focus. In the normal (or emmetropic) eye, the region where the rays of light converge to a point corresponds with the retina.

The greatest change of direction, or bending of the rays, occurs where the difference of refractive index is greatest, and this is when light passes from air into the cornea, the refractive index of the corneal substance being 1.3376; the refractive indices of the cornea and aqueous humour are not greatly different, that of the aqueous humour being 1.336 (as is that of the vitreous); thus, the bending, as the rays meet the concave posterior surface of the cornea and emerge into a medium of slightly less refractive index, is small. The lens has a greater refractive index than that of its surrounding aqueous humour and vitreous body, 1.386 to 1.406, so that its two surfaces contribute to convergence, the posterior surface normally more than the anterior surface because of its greater curvature (smaller radius).

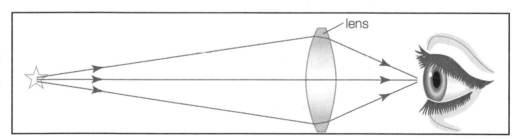

A double convex lens, or converging lens, focuses the diverging, or blurred, light rays from a distant object by refracting (bending) the rays twice. At the front side of the lens, the rays are bent toward the normal (the perpendicular to the surface) because the glass is a denser medium than the air, and, at the back side of the lens, the rays are bent away from the normal as the rays pass into the less-dense medium of the air. This double bending causes the rays to converge at a focal point behind the lens so that a sharper image can be seen or photographed. Encyclopædia Britannica, Inc.

FOCUSING

Focusing, also called ocular accommodation, is the ability of the lens to alter its shape to allow objects to be seen clearly. In humans, the forward surface of the lens is made more convex for seeing objects up close. At the same time, the pupil becomes smaller, and the two eyes turn inward (i.e., cross or converge) to the point that their gaze is fixed on the object. The capsule, or envelope enclosing the lens of the eye, is attached by suspensory ligaments (called zonular fibres) to the ringlike ciliary muscle that encircles the lens. The inside diameter of this muscle is greatest when the muscle is relaxed and smallest when the muscle is contracted. Thus, when the gaze is fixed on a distant object, as when a camera is set at infinity, the ciliary muscle relaxes, the muscle's inside diameter is increased, more pull is exerted on the lens by the ligaments, and the front surface of the lens is flattened. When near objects are viewed, the ciliary muscle contracts, the ligaments relax, and the lens, being elastic, bulges in front and gains more curvature. This increased curvature enhances the focusing power of the lens and brings the nearer object to better focus on the retina. This process, known as accommodation, is controlled by parasympathetic fibres of the third (oculomotor) cranial nerve. As a person ages, the lens hardens and slowly loses its ability to change shape and bring near objects into better focus. This condition is called presbyopia and generally becomes evident after age 40.

ABNORMALITIES OF FOCUS

In contrast to the focussing of the normal eye, in which the image of the visual field is focussed on the retina, the image may be focussed in front of the retina (nearsightedness, or myopia), or behind the retina (farsightedness or hyperopia). In myopia the vision of distant objects is not distinct because the image of a distant point falls within the vitreous and the rays spread out to form a blur circle on the retina instead of a point. In this condition the eye is said to have too great dioptric (refractive) power for its length. When the focus falls behind the retina, the image of the distant point is again a circle on the retina; and the farsighted eye is said to have too little dioptric power.

The important point to appreciate is that emmetropia, or normal sight, requires that the focal power of the dioptric system be matched to the axial length of the eye; it certainly is remarkable that emmetropia is indeed the most common condition when it is appreciated that just one millimetre of error in the matching of axial length with focal length would cause a person to require visual correction with contact lenses or eyeglasses. In general, however, the effects of variations in dimensions tend to compensate each other. Thus, for example, an unusually large eye might, at first thought, be expected to be myopic, but a large eye tends to be associated with a large radius of curvature of the cornea, and this would reduce the power—i.e., increase the focal length—and so an unusually large eye is not necessarily a myopic one.

ACCOMMODATION

The image of an object brought close to the eye would be formed behind the retina if there were no change in the focal length of the eye. This change to bring the image of an object upon the retina is called accommodation. The point nearer than which accommodation is no longer effective is called the near point of accommodation. In very young people, the near point of accommodation is quite close to the eye, namely about 7 cm (about 3 inches) in front at age 10; at age 40 the distance has increased to about 16 cm (about 6 inches), and at age 60 it can be as distant as 100 cm (39 inches). Thus, a 60-year-old may not be able to read a book held at the convenient distance of about 40 cm (16 inches), and the extra power required would have to be provided by convex lenses in front of the eye, an arrangement called the presbyopic correction.

Mechanism of Accommodation

It is essentially an increase in curvature of the anterior surface of the lens that is responsible for the increase in power involved in the process of accommodation. A clue to the way in which this change in shape takes place is given by the observation that a lens that has been taken out of the eye is much rounder and fatter than one within the eye; thus, its attachments by the zonular fibres to the ciliary muscle within the eye preserve the unaccommodated or flattened state of the lens; and modern investigations leave little doubt that it is the pull of the zonular fibres on the elastic capsule of the lens that holds the anterior surface relatively flat. When these zonular fibres are loosened, the elastic tension in the capsule comes into play and remolds the lens, making it smaller and thicker. Thus, the physiological problem is to find what loosens the zonular fibres during accommodation.

The contraction of the fibres of the ciliary muscle function to pull the whole ciliary body forward and to move the anterior region toward the axis of the eye by virtue of the sphincter action of the circular fibres. Both of these actions will slacken the zonular fibres and therefore allow the change in shape. As to why it is the anterior surface that changes most is not absolutely clear, but it is probably a characteristic of the capsule rather than of the underlying lens tissue.

Nerve Action of Accommodation

Accommodation is an involuntary reflex act, and the ciliary muscle belongs to the smooth involuntary class. Appropriate to this, the innervation is through the autonomic system, the parasympathetic nerve cells belonging to the oculomotor nerve (the third cranial nerve) occupying a special region of the nucleus in the midbrain called the Edinger-Westphal nucleus; the fibres have a relay point in the ciliary ganglion in the eye socket, and the postganglionic fibres enter the eye as the short ciliary nerves. The stimulus for accommodation is the nearness of the object, but the manner in which this nearness is translated into a stimulus is not clear. Thus, the fact that the image is blurred is not sufficient to induce accommodation; the eye has some power of discriminating whether the blurredness is due to an object being too far away or too close, so that something more than mere blurredness is required.

PUPIL RESPONSE

The amount of light entering the eye is restricted by the aperture in the iris, the pupil. When a person is in a dark room his or her pupil is large, perhaps 8 mm (0.3 inch) in diameter, or more. When the room is lighted there is an immediate constriction of the pupil, the light reflex; this is bilateral, so that even if only one eye is exposed to the light both pupils contract to nearly the same extent. After a time the pupils expand even though the bright light is maintained, but the expansion is not large. The final state is determined by the actual degree of illumination; if this is high, then the final state may be a diameter of only about 3 to 4 mm (about 0.15 inch); if it is not so high, then the initial constriction may be nearly the same, but the final state may be with a pupil of 4 to 5 mm (about 0.18 inch). During

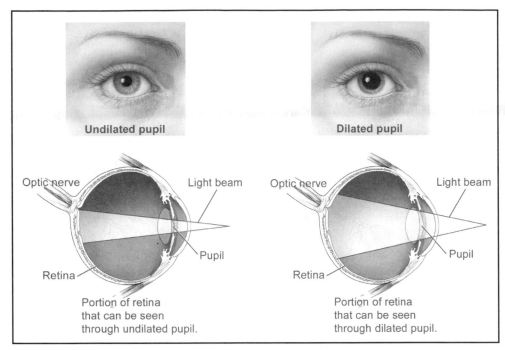

This diagram shows pupils before and after they are dilated. National Eye Institute, National Institutes of Health

this steady condition, the pupils do not remain at exactly constant size; there is a characteristic oscillation in size that, if exaggerated, is called hippus.

A pupillary constriction will also occur when a person looks at a near object—the near reflex. Thus, accommodation and pupillary constriction occur together reflexly and are excited by the same stimulus. The function of the pupil is clearly that of controlling the amount of light entering the eye, and hence the light reflex. The constriction occurring during near vision suggests other functions, too; thus, the aberrations of the eye (failure of some refracted rays to focus on the retina) are decreased by reducing the aperture of its optical system. In the dark, aberrations are of negligible significance, so that a person is concerned only with allowing as much light into the eye as possible; in bright light high visual acuity is usually required, and this means reducing the aberrations. The depth of focus of the optical system is increased when the aperture is reduced, and the near reflex is probably concerned with increasing depth of focus under these conditions.

Dilation of the pupil occurs as a result of strong psychical stimuli and also when any sensory nerve is stimulated; dilation thus occurs in extreme fear and in pain. Dilation is brought about by the shortening of the radially oriented fibres of the dilator muscle of the iris. The dilator muscle is activated by sympathetic nerve fibres. Stimulation of the sympathetic nerve in the neck causes a powerful dilation of the iris; the influx of adrenalin into the blood from the adrenal glands during extreme excitement results in pupillary dilation.

The muscle fibres that form the circular sphincter muscle of the iris function to constrict the pupil and work by shortening; this action reduces the size of the aperture and thereby restricts the amount of light entering the eye. The sphincter is innervated by parasympathetic fibres of the oculomotor nerve, with their cell bodies in the Edinger-Westphal nucleus, as are the nerve cells controlling accommodation; thus, the close association between the accommodation and pupillary reflexes is reflected in a close anatomical contiguity of their motor nerve cells.

The sensory pathway in the light reflex involves the rods and cones, bipolar cells, and ganglion cells. A relay centre for pupillary responses to light is the pretectal nucleus in the midbrain. There is a partial crossing-over of the fibres of the pretectal nerve cells so that some may run to the motor nerve cells in the Edinger-Westphal nucleus of both sides of the brain, and it is by this means that illumination of one eye affects the other. The

Edinger-Westphal motor neurons have a relay point in the ciliary ganglion, a group of nerve cells in the eye socket, so that its electrical stimulation causes both accommodation and pupillary constriction; similarly, application of a drug, such as pilocarpine, to the cornea will cause a constriction of the pupil and also a spasm of accommodation; atropine, by paralyzing the nerve supply, causes dilation of the pupil and paralysis of accommodation (cycloplegia).

Many involuntary muscles receive a double innervation, being activated by one type of nerve supply and inhibited by the other; the iris muscles are no exception — the sphincter has an inhibitory sympathetic nerve supply, while the dilator has an inhibitory parasympathetic (cholinergic) nerve supply. Thus, a drug like pilocarpine not only activates the constrictor muscle but actively inhibits the dilator. A similar double innervation has been described for the ciliary muscle. In general, any change in pupillary size results from a reciprocal innervation of dilator and constrictor; thus, activation of the constrictor is associated with inhibition of the dilator and vice versa.

In general, pupillary constriction and accommodation occur together, in response to the same stimulus; a third element in this near response is, of course, the convergence (turning in) of the eyes, mediated by voluntary muscles, the medial recti. Experimentally, it is often possible to separate these activities, in the sense that one may cause convergence without accommodation by placing appropriate prisms in front of the eyes; or one may cause accommodation without convergence by placing diverging lenses in front of the eyes. There are many experiments that show that accommodation and convergence are neurologically linked to some extent, however.

CHAPTER 3
VISION AND THE RETINA

The retina is fundamental to vision. It contains millions of light-sensitive photoreceptors that are essential to the perception of visual information. The photoreceptors of the human eye are assembled into complex networks of neurons that serve to organize incoming visual information into messages that can be interpreted by the brain.

In the retina, as in other parts of the nervous system, the messages initiated in one element are transmitted, or relayed, to others. The regions of transmission from one cell to another are areas of intimate contact known as synapses. An impulse conveyed from one cell to another travels from the first cell body along a projection called an axon, to a synapse, where the impulse is received by a projection, called a dendrite, of the second cell. The impulse is then conveyed to the second cell body, to be transmitted further, along the second cell's axon. Impulses are eventually transmitted to the optic nerve, which in turn carries the impulses to the visual centres of the brain. In this way, through the systematic transmission of electrical impulses along neurons, the information received by the retina is converted into a meaningful image.

NEURON NETWORKS
OF THE RETINA

The functioning cells of the retina include the photoreceptors—the rods and cones; the ganglion cells, the axons

STRUCTURE OF THE RETINA

optic nerve fiber

ganglion cell

bipolar neuron

rod cell

cone cell

pigmented epithelium

A diagram of the structure of the retina. Conditions affecting the retina can impair both central visual acuity and peripheral vision as well as alter light detection and image perception. Copyright Encyclopaedia Britannica; rendering for this edition by Rosen Educational Services.

of which form the optic nerve; and cells that act in a variety of ways as intermediaries between the receptors and the ganglion cells. These intermediaries are named bipolar cells, horizontal cells, and amacrine cells.

The synapses between these cells occur in definite layers, the outer and inner plexiform layers. In the outer plexiform layer the bipolar cells make their contacts, by way of their dendrites, with the rods and cones, specifically the spherules of the rods and the pedicles of the cones. In this layer, too, the projections from horizontal cells make contacts with rods, cones, and bipolar cells, giving rise to a horizontal transmission and thereby allowing activity in one part of the retina to influence the behaviour of a neighbouring part. In the inner plexiform layer, the axons of the bipolar cells make connection with the dendrites of ganglion cells, once again at special synaptic regions. (The dendrites of a nerve cell carry impulses to the nerve cell body; its axon, away from the cell body.) Here, too, a horizontal interconnection between bipolar cells is brought about, in this case by way of the axons and dendrites of amacrine cells.

The bipolar cells are of two main types: namely, those that apparently make connection with only one receptor—a cone—and those that connect to several receptors. The type of bipolar cell that connects to a single cone is called the midget bipolar. The other type of bipolar cell is called diffuse; varieties of these include the rod bipolar, the dendritic projections of which spread over an area wide enough to allow contacts with as many as 50 rods; and the flat cone bipolar, which collects messages from up to seven cones. Ganglion cells are of two main types: namely, the midget ganglion cell, which apparently makes a unique connection with a midget bipolar cell, which in turn is directly connected to a single cone; and a diffuse type, which collects messages from groups of bipolar cells.

The presence of diffuse bipolar and ganglion cells collecting messages from groups of receptors and bipolar cells, and, what may be even more important, the presence of lateral connections of groups of receptors and bipolar cells through the horizontal and amacrine cells, means that messages from receptors over a rather large area of the retina may converge on a single ganglion cell. This convergence means that the effects of light falling on the receptive field may be cumulative, so that a weak light stimulus spread over about 1,000 rods is just as effective as a stronger stimulus spread over 100 or less; in other words, a large receptive field will have a lower threshold than a small one; and this is, in fact, the basis for the high sensitivity of the area immediately outside the fovea, where there is a high density of rods that converge on single bipolar cells. Thus, if it is postulated that the cones do not converge to anything like the same extent as the rods, the greater sensitivity of the latter may be explained; and the anatomical evidence favours this postulate.

The regeneration of visual pigment is a cause of the increased sensitivity of the rods that occurs during dark adaptation. This, apparently, is only part of the story. An important additional factor is the change in functional organization of the retina during adaptation. When the eye is light-adapted, functional convergence is small, and sensitivity of rods and cones is low; as dark adaptation proceeds, convergence of rods increases. The anatomical connections do not change, but the power of the bipolar cells and ganglion cells to collect impulses is increased, perhaps by the removal of an inhibition that prevents this during high illumination of the retina.

THE WORK OF THE RETINA

The structure of the retina and its relation to chemically identifiable events provides some indication of the work that the retina must perform in order for image generation to be successful. Factors such as threshold stimulus, dark adaptation, and bleaching affect the electrophysiological response of the retina to light and thus ultimately impact the relay of visual messages to the brain.

THRESHOLD OF LIGHT DETECTION

An important means of measuring a sensation is to determine the threshold stimulus—i.e., the minimum energy required to evoke the sensation. In the case of vision, this would be the minimum number of quanta of light entering the eye in unit time. If it is found that the threshold has altered because of a change of some sort, then this change can be said to have altered the subject's sensitivity to light, and a numerical value can be assigned to the sensitivity by use of the reciprocal of the threshold energy.

Practically, a subject may be placed in the dark in front of a white screen, and the screen may be illuminated by flashes of light; for any given intensity of illumination of the screen, it is not difficult to calculate the flow of light energy entering the eye. One may begin with a low intensity of flash and increase this successively until the subject reports that he or she can see the flash. In fact, at this threshold level, the subject will not see every flash presented, even though the intensity of the light is kept constant; for this reason, a certain frequency of seeing— e.g., four times out of six—must be selected as the arbitrary point at which to fix the threshold.

When different wavelengths of light are employed for measuring the threshold, it is found that the eye is much more sensitive to blue-green light than to orange. The interesting feature of this kind of study is that the subject reports only that the light is light; he or she distinguishes no colour. If the intensity of a given wavelength of light is increased step by step above the threshold, a point comes when the subject states that it is coloured, and the difference between the threshold for light appreciation and this, the chromatic threshold, is called the photochromatic interval. This suggests that the rods give only achromatic, or colourless, vision, and that it is the cones that permit wavelength discrimination. The photochromatic interval for long wavelengths (red light) is about zero, which means that the intensity required to reach the sensation of light is the same as that to reach the sensation of colour. This is because the rods are so insensitive to red light; if the dark-adaptation curve is plotted for a red stimulus it is found that it follows the cone path, like that for foveal vision at all wavelengths.

DARK ADAPTATION

The threshold for light detection falls progressively over the course of minutes when a person keeps his or her eyes open in a dark room. This is not due to dilation of the pupil because the same phenomenon occurs if the person is made to look through an artificial pupil of fixed diameter. The eye, after about 30 minutes in the dark, may become about 10,000 times more sensitive to light. Vision under these conditions is, moreover, characteristically different from what it is under ordinary daylight conditions. Thus, in studies in which a subject is placed in a dark room in front of a screen illuminated by flashes, the eye obtains its best vision when looking away from the screen so that the image of the screen does not fall on the fovea; if the screen is continuously illuminated at around this threshold level it will be found to disappear if its image is brought onto the fovea, and it will become immediately visible on looking away. The same phenomenon may be demonstrated on a moonless night if the gaze is fixed on a dim star; it disappears on fixation and reappears on looking away. This feature of vision under these near-threshold or scotopic (dark-adapted) conditions suggests that the cones are effectively blind to weak light stimuli, since they are the only receptors in the fovea. This is the basis of the duplicity theory of vision, which postulates that when the light stimulus is weak and the eye has been dark-adapted, it is the rods that are utilized because, under these conditions, their threshold is much lower than that of the cones. When the subject first enters the dark, the rods are the less sensitive type of receptor, and the threshold stimulus is the light energy required to stimulate the cones; during the first five or more minutes the threshold of the cones decreases; i.e., they become more sensitive. The rods then increase their sensitivity to the point that they are the more sensitive, and it is they that now determine the sensitivity of the whole eye, the threshold stimuli obtained after 10 minutes in the dark, for example, being too weak to activate the cones.

If, when the subject has become completely dark-adapted, one eye is held shut and the other exposed to a bright light for a little while, it is found that, whereas the dark-adapted eye retains its high sensitivity, that of the light-exposed eye has decreased greatly; it requires another period of dark adaptation for the two eyes to become equally sensitive.

These simple experiments pose several problems, the answers to which throw a great deal of light on the whole mechanism of vision. Why, for example, does it require time for both rods and cones to reach their maximum sensitivity in the dark? Again, why is visual acuity so low under dark-adapted conditions compared with that in daylight, although sensitivity to light is so high? Finally, why do the rods not serve to discriminate different wavelengths?

BLEACHING

It may be assumed that a receptor is sensitive to light because it contains a substance that absorbs light and converts this vibrational type of energy into some other form that is eventually transmuted into electrical changes, and that these may be transmitted from the receptor to the bipolar cell with which it is immediately connected. When the retina of a dark-adapted animal is removed and submitted to extraction procedures, a pigment, originally called visual purple but now called rhodopsin, may be obtained. If the eye is exposed to a bright light for some time before extraction, little or no rhodopsin is obtained.

When retinas from animals that had been progressively dark-adapted were studied, a gradual increase in the amount of rhodopsin that could be extracted was observed. Thus, rhodopsin, on absorption of light energy, is changed to some other compound, but new rhodopsin is formed, or rhodopsin is regenerated, during dark adaptation. The obvious inference is that rhodopsin is the visual pigment of the rods, and that when it is exposed to relatively intense lights it becomes useless for vision. When the eye is allowed to remain in the dark the rhodopsin regenerates and thus becomes available for vision. There is conclusive proof that rhodopsin is, indeed, the visual pigment for the rods; it is obtained from retinas that have only rods and no cones—e.g., the retinas of the rat or guinea pig, and it is not obtained from the pure cone retina of the chicken.

When the absorption spectrum is measured, it is found that its maximum absorption occurs at the point of maximum sensitivity of the dark-adapted eye. Similar measurements may be carried out on animals, but the threshold sensitivity must be determined by some objective means—e.g., the response of the pupil, or, better still, the electrical changes occurring in the retina in response to light stimuli. Thus, the electroretinogram (ERG) is the record of changes in potential between an electrode placed on the surface of the cornea and an electrode placed on another part of the body, caused by illumination of the eye.

The high sensitivity of the rods by comparison with the cones may be a reflection of the greater concentration in them of pigment that would permit them to catch light more efficiently, or it may depend on other factors—e.g., the efficiency of transformation of the light energy into electrical energy. An important factor, so far as sensitivity is concerned, is the actual organization of the receptors and neurons in the retina.

MINIMUM STIMULUS FOR VISION

The minimum threshold for vision is best indicated in terms of frequency of seeing since, because of fluctuations in the threshold, there is no definite luminance (brightness of light) of a test screen at which it is always seen by the observer, and there is no luminance just below this at which it is never seen. Experiments, in which 60 percent was arbitrarily taken as the frequency of seeing and in which the image of a patch of light covered an area of retina containing about 20,000,000 rods, led to the calculation that the mean threshold stimulus represents 2,500 quanta of light that is actually absorbed per square centimetre of retina. This calculation leads to two important conclusions: namely, that at the threshold only one rod out of thousands comes into operation, and that during the application of a short stimulus the chances are that no rod receives more than a single quantum.

A quantum, defined as the product of Planck's constant (6.63×10^{-27} erg-second) times the frequency of light, is the minimum amount of light energy that can be employed. A rod excited by a single quantum cannot excite a bipolar cell without the simultaneous assistance of one or more other rods. Experiments carried out in the 1940s indicated that a stimulus of about 11 quanta is required; thus it may require 11 excited rods, each receiving one quantum of light, to produce the sensation of light.

Quantum Fluctuations

With such small amounts of energy as those involved in the threshold stimulus, the uncertainty principle becomes important; according to this, there is no certainty that a given flash will have the expected number of quanta in it, but only a probability. Thus, one may speak of a certain average number of quanta and the actual number in any given flash, and one may compute on statistical grounds the shape of curve that is obtained by plotting frequency with which a flash contains, say, four quanta or more against the average number in the flash. One may also plot the frequency with which a flash is seen against the average number of quanta in the flash, and this frequency-of-seeing curve turns out to be similar to the frequency-of-containing-quanta curve when the number of quanta chosen is five to seven, depending on the observer. This congruence strongly suggests that the fluctuations in response to a flash of the same average intensity are caused by fluctuations in the energy content of the stimulus, and not by fluctuations in the sensitivity of the retina.

Spatial Summation

In spatial summation two stimuli falling on nearby areas of the retina add their effects so that either alone may be inadequate to evoke the sensation of light, but, when presented simultaneously, they may do so. Thus, the threshold luminance of a test patch required to be just visible depends, within limits, on its size, a larger patch requiring a lower luminance, and vice versa. Within a small range of limiting area, namely that subtending about 10 to 15 minutes of arc, the relationship called Ricco's law holds; i.e., threshold intensity multiplied by the area equals a constant. This means that over this area, which embraces several hundreds of rods, light falling on the individual rods summates, or accumulates, its effects completely so that 100 quanta falling on a single rod are as effective as one quantum falling simultaneously on 100 rods. The basis for this summation is clearly the convergence of receptors on ganglion cells, the chemical effects of the quanta of light falling on individual rods being converted into electrical changes that converge on a single bipolar cell through its branching dendritic processes. Again, the electrical effects induced in the bipolar cells may summate at the dendritic processes of a ganglion cell so that the receptive field of a ganglion cell may embrace many thousands of rods.

Temporal Summation

In temporal summation, two stimuli, each being too weak to excite, cause a sensation of light if presented in rapid succession on the same spot of the retina; thus, over a certain range of times, up to 0.1 second, the Bunsen-Roscoe law holds: namely, that the intensity of light multiplied by the time of exposure equals a constant. Thus it was found that within this time interval (up to 0.1 second), the total number of quanta required to excite vision was 130, irrespective of the manner in which these were supplied. Beyond this time, summation was still evident, but it was not perfect, so that if the duration was increased to one second the total number of quanta required was 220. Temporal summation is consistent with quantum theory; it has been shown that fluctuations in the number of quanta actually in a light flash are responsible for the variable responsiveness of the eye; increasing the duration of a light stimulus increases the probability that it will contain a given number of quanta, and that it will excite.

INHIBITION

In the central nervous system generally, the relay of impulses from one nerve cell or neuron to excite another is only one aspect of neuronal interaction. Just as important, if not more so, is the inhibition of one neuron by the discharge in another. So it is in the retina. Subjectively, the inhibitory activity is reflected in many of the phenomena associated with adaptation to light or its reverse. Thus, the decrease in sensitivity of the retina to light during exposure to light is only partially accounted for by bleaching of visual pigment, be it the pigment in rod or cone; an important factor is the onset of inhibitory processes that reduce the convergence of receptors on ganglion cells. Some of the rapidly occurring changes in sensitivity described as alpha adaptation are doubtless purely neural in origin.

Many so-called inductive phenomena indicate inhibitory processes; thus, the phenomenon of simultaneous contrast, whereby a patch of light appears much darker if surrounded by a bright background than by a black, is due to the inhibitory effect of the surrounding retina on the central region, induced by the bright surrounding. Many colour-contrast phenomena are similarly caused; thus, if a blue light is projected onto a large white screen, the white screen rapidly appears yellow; the blue stimulus falling on the central retina causes inhibition of blue sensitivity in the periphery; hence, the white background will appear to be missing its blue light—white minus blue is a mixture of red and green, which appears as yellow to the retina. Particularly interesting from this viewpoint are the phenomena of metacontrast; by this is meant the inductive effect of a primary light stimulus on the sensitivity of the eye to a previously presented light stimulus on an adjoining area of retina. It is a combination of temporal and spatial induction. The effect is produced by illuminating the two halves of a circular patch consecutively for a brief duration. If the left half only, for example, is illuminated for 10 milliseconds it produces a definite sensation of brightness. If both halves are illuminated for the same period, but the right half from 20 to 50 milliseconds later, the left half of the field appears much darker than before and, near the centre, may be completely extinguished. The left field has thus been inhibited by the succeeding, nearby, stimulus. The right field, moreover, appears darker than when illuminated alone—it has been inhibited by the earlier stimulus (paracontrast).

FLICKER

Another visual phenomenon that brings out the importance of inhibition is the sensation evoked when a visual stimulus is repeated rapidly; for example, one may view a screen that is illuminated by a source of light the rays from which may be intercepted at regular intervals by rotating a sector of a circular screen in front of it. If the sector rotates slowly, a sensation of black followed by white is aroused; as the speed increases the sensation becomes one of flicker—i.e., rapid fluctuations in brightness; finally, at a certain speed, called the critical fusion frequency, the sensation becomes continuous and the subject is unaware of the alterations in the illumination of the screen.

At high levels of luminance, when cone vision is employed, the fusion frequency is high, increasing with increasing luminance in a logarithmic fashion—the Ferry-Porter law—so that at high levels it may require 60 flashes per second to reach a continuous sensation. Under conditions of night, or scotopic, vision, the frequencies may be as low as four per second. The difference between rod and cone vision in this respect probably resides in the power of the eye to inhibit activity in cones rapidly, so that the sensation evoked by a single flash is cut off immediately, and this leaves the eye ready to respond to the next stimulus. By contrast, the response in the rod lasts so much longer that, when a new stimulus falls even a quarter of a second later, the difference in the state of the rods is insufficient to evoke a change in intensity of sensation; it merely prolongs it.

One interesting feature of an intermittent stimulus is that the intensity of the sensation of brightness, when fusion is achieved, is dependent on the relative periods of light and darkness in the cycle, and this gives one a method of grading the effective luminance of a screen; one may keep the intensity of the illuminating source constant and merely vary the period of blackness in a cycle of black and white. The effective luminance will be the average luminance during a cycle; this is known as the Talbot-Plateau law.

VISUAL ACUITY

The ability to perceive detail is restricted in the dark-adapted retina when the illumination is such as to excite only the scotopic type of vision; this is in spite of the high sensitivity of the retina to light under the same conditions. The power of distinguishing detail is essentially the power to resolve two stimuli separated in space, so that, if a grating of black lines on a white background is moved farther and farther away from an observer, a point is reached when he or she will be unable to distinguish this stimulus pattern from a uniformly gray sheet of paper.

The angle subtended at the eye by the spacing between the lines at the point where they are just resolvable is called the resolving power of the eye; the reciprocal of this angle, in minutes of arc, is called the visual acuity. Thus, a visual acuity of unity indicates a power of resolving detail subtending one minute of arc at the eye; a visual acuity of two indicates a resolution of one-half minute, or 30 seconds of arc. The visual acuity depends strongly on the illumination of the test target, and this is true of both daylight (photopic) and night (scotopic) vision; thus, with a brightly illuminated target, with the surroundings equally brightly illuminated (the ideal condition), the visual acuity may be as high as two. When the illumination is reduced, the acuity falls so that, under ordinary conditions of daylight viewing, visual acuity is not much better than unity. Under scotopic conditions, the visual acuity may be only 0.04 so that lines would have to subtend about 25 minutes at the eye to be resolvable; this corresponds to a thickness of 4.4 cm (1.7 inches) at a distance of 6 metres (20 feet).

In the laboratory, visual acuity is measured by the Landolt C, which is a circle with a break in it. The subject is asked to state where the break is when the figure is rotated to successive random positions. The size of the C, and thus of its break, is reduced until the subject makes more than an arbitrarily chosen percentage of mistakes. The angle subtended at the eye by the break in the C at this limit is taken as the resolving power of the eye. The

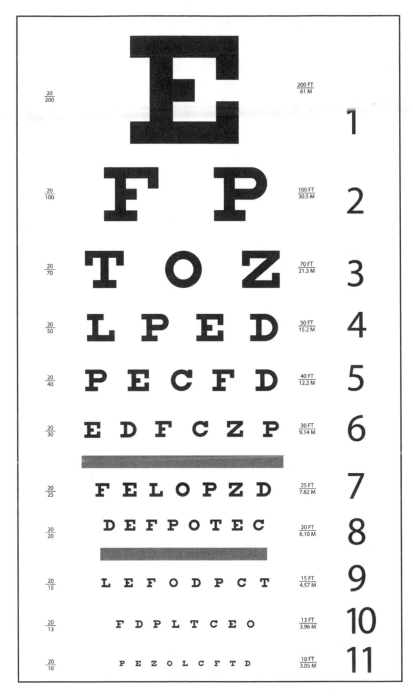

Doctors use the Snellen eye chart to check vision. Shutterstock.com

testing of the eyes by the ophthalmologist or optometrist is essentially a determination of visual acuity; here the subject is presented with the Snellen chart, rows of letters whose details subtend progressively smaller angles at the eye. The row in which, say, five out of six letters are seen correctly is chosen as that which measures the visual acuity. If the details subtended one minute of arc, the visual acuity would be unity. The notation employed is somewhat obscure; a visual acuity of unity would be expressed as 6/6; an acuity of a half as 6/12, and so on; here the numerator is the viewing distance in metres from the chart and the denominator the distance at which details on the letters of the limiting row subtend one minute of arc at the eye.

Retinal Design and Visual Acuity

From an anatomical point of view one may expect the limit to resolving power to be imposed by the "grain" of the retinal mosaic in the same way that the size of the grains in a photographic emulsion imposes a limit to the accuracy with which detail may be photographed. Two white lines on a black ground, for example, could not be appreciated as distinct if their images fell on the same or adjacent sets of receptors. If a set of receptors intervened between the stimulated ones, there would be a basis for discrimination because the message sent to the central nervous system could be that two rows of receptors, separated by an unstimulated row, were sending messages to their bipolar cells. Thus, the limit to resolution, on this basis, should be the diameter of a foveal cone, or rather the angle subtended by this at the nodal point of the eye; this is about 30 seconds of arc and, in fact, corresponds with the best visual acuity attainable. If this grain of the retinal mosaic is to be the basis of resolution, however, one must postulate, in addition, a nervous mechanism that will transmit accurately the events taking place in the individual receptors, in this case the foveal cones; i.e., there must be a one-to-one relationship between cones, bipolar cells, ganglion cells, and lateral geniculate cells so that what is called the local sign of the impulses from a given foveal cone may be obtained.

It must be appreciated that restriction on convergence (or its reverse, spread) of messages may be achieved by inhibition; the anatomical connections may be there, but they may be made functionally inoperative by inhibition exerted by other neurons; thus, the horizontal and amacrine cells might well exert a restraining influence on certain junctions, thereby reducing the spread, or convergence, of messages, and it seems likely that the improvement in foveal visual acuity from one to two, brought about by increased luminance of the target and its surroundings, is achieved by an increase in inhibition that tends to make transmission one-to-one in the fovea.

True one-to-one connections in the retina do not exist; a cone, although making an exclusive type of synapse with a midget bipolar, may also make a less exclusive contact with a flat bipolar cell; furthermore, midget bipolars and cones are connected laterally by amacrine and horizontal cells so that it is most unlikely that a given optic nerve fibre carries messages from only a single cone. The one-to-one relationship may in fact exist under certain conditions, but that is because pathways from other receptors have been blocked or occluded by inhibitory processes that keep the line clear for a given cone.

A high sensitivity to light is achieved by the convergence of rods on the higher neurons to allow spatial summation, and it is this convergence that interferes with the resolution of detail. If hundreds of rods converge on a single bipolar cell and if many bipolar cells converge on a single ganglion cell, it is understandable that the unit responsible for resolution may be very large and thus that the visual acuity is very small.

The Retinal Image

The limiting factor of visual acuity is one of an anatomical arrangement of receptors and of their neural organization. A very important feature, however, must be the accuracy of the formation of an image of external objects by the optical system of the eye. It may be calculated, for example, that the image of a grating produces lines 0.5 micrometre wide on the retina, but this is on the basis of ideal geometrical optics; in fact, the optics of the eye are not perfect, while diffraction of light by its passage through the pupil further spoils the image. As a result of these defects, the image of a black and white grating on the retina is not sharp, the black lines being not completely black but gray because of spread of light from the white lines. (When the optical system of the eye is defective, moreover, as in nearsightedness, the imagery is worse, but this can be corrected by the use of appropriate lenses.)

Physiologically, the eye effectively improves the retinal image by enhancing contrasts; thus, the image of a fine black line on a white background formed on the retina is not a sharply defined black line but a relatively wide band of varying degrees of grayness; yet to the observer the line appears sharply defined, and this is because of lateral inhibition, the receptors that receive most light tending to inhibit those that receive less; the result is a physiological "sharpening of the image," so that the eye often behaves as though the image were perfect. This applies to chromatic aberration, too, which should cause black and white objects to appear fringed with colour, yet, because of suppression of the chromatic responses, one is not aware of the coloured fringes that do in effect surround the images of objects in the external world.

The iris behaves as a diaphragm, modifying the amount of light entering the eye; probably of greater significance than control of the light entering the eye is the influence on aberrations of the optical system; the smaller the pupil the less serious, in general, are the aberrations. The smaller the pupil, however, the more serious become the effects of diffraction, so that a balance must be struck. Experimentally, it is found that at high luminances with pupils below 3 mm (0.12 inch) in diameter the visual acuity is not improved by further reduction of the diameter; increasing the pupil size beyond this reduces acuity, presumably because of the greater optical aberrations.

When a subject is placed in a room that is darkened steadily, the size of the pupil increases, and the size attained for any given level of luminance is, in fact, optimal for visual acuity at this particular luminance. The reason that visual acuity increases with the larger pupils is that the extra light admitted into the eye compensates for the increased aberrations. When the gaze is fixed intently on an object for a long time, peripheral images that tend to disappear reappear immediately when the eyes are moved. This effect is called the Troxler phenomenon. To study it reproducibly it is necessary to use an optical device that ensures that the image of any object upon which the gaze is fixed will remain on the same part of the retina however the eyes move. Investigations using this method have revealed that the stabilized retinal image tends to fade within a few seconds. It may be assumed that in normal vision the normal involuntary movements—microsaccades and drifts—keep the retinal image in sufficient movement to prevent fading, which is essentially an example of sensory adaptation, the tendency for any receptive system to cease responding to a maintained stimulus.

CHAPTER 4

ELECTROPHYSIOLOGY OF THE RETINA

S tudies of the electrophysiological activity of the retina
have provided valuable information about the neurological organization of the human eye. Because subjective
studies on humans can traverse only a certain distance in
the interpretation of visual phenomena, electrophysiological techniques, which have been successful in unravelling
the mechanisms of the central nervous system, must be
applied to the eye. These techniques, which centre on the
use of electrodes to measure electrical impulses of neurons, contributed to a significant expansion in scientists'
knowledge of the neural activity of the human eye in the
20th and early 21st centuries.

NEUROLOGICAL BASIS

Records from single optic nerve fibres of the frog and
from the ganglion cell of the mammalian retina have indicated that there are three types of neural response. In the
frog there are fibres that give a discharge when a light is
switched on; these are known as the "on-fibres." Another
group, the "off-fibres," remain inactive during illumination of the retina but give a powerful discharge when a
light is switched off. A third group, the "on-off fibres," give
discharges at "on" and "off" but are inactive during illumination. The responses in the mammal are similar, but more
complex than in the frog. The mammalian retina shows a
background of activity in the dark, so that on- and

off-effects are manifest as accentuations or diminutions of this normal discharge. In general, on-elements give an increased discharge when a light is switched on, and an inhibition of the background discharge when the light is switched off. An off-element shows inhibition of the background discharge during illumination and a powerful discharge at off; this off-discharge is thus a release of inhibition and reveals unmistakably the inhibitory character of the response to illumination that takes place in some ganglion cells. Each ganglion cell or optic nerve fibre has a receptive field; and the area of frog's retina from which a single fibre is activated varies with the intensity of the light stimulus. The largest field is obtained with the strongest stimulus.

The mammalian receptive field is more complex, the more peripheral part of the field giving the opposite type of response to that given by the centre. Thus, if, at the centre of the field, a response is "on" (an on-centre field), the response to a stimulus farther away in the same fibre is at "off," and in an intermediate zone it is often mixed to give an on-off element. In order to characterize an element, therefore, it must be called on-centre or off-centre, with the meaning thereby that at the centre of its receptive field its response is at "on" or at "off," respectively, while in the periphery it is opposite. Studies of the effects of small spot stimuli on centre and periphery separately and together have demonstrated a mutual inhibition between the two. A striking feature is the effect of adaptation; after dark adaptation the surrounding area of opposite activity becomes ineffective. In this sense, therefore, the receptive field shrinks, but, as it is a reduction in inhibitory activity between centre and periphery, it means, in fact, that the effective field can actually increase during dark adaptation—i.e., the regions over which summation can occur—and this is exactly what is found in psychophysical experiments on dark adaptation.

The receptive field is essentially a measure of the number of receptors — rods or cones or a mixture of these — that make nervous connections with a single ganglion cell. The organization of centre and periphery implies that the receptors in the periphery of an on-centre cell tend to inhibit it, while those in the centre of the field tend to excite it, so that the effects of a uniform illumination covering the whole field tend to cancel out. This has an important physiological value, as it means, in effect, that the brain is not bombarded with an enormous number of unnecessary messages, as would be the case were every ganglion cell to send discharges along its optic nerve fibre as long as it was illuminated. Instead, the cell tends to respond to change—i.e., the movement of a light or dark spot over the receptive field—and to give an especially prominent response, often when the spot passes from the periphery to the centre, or vice versa. Thus, the centre-periphery organization favours the detection of movement; in a similar way it favours the detection of contours because these give rise to differences in the illumination of the parts of the receptive fields.

The anatomical basis of the arrangement presumably is given by the organization of the bipolar and amacrine cells in relation to the dendrites of the ganglion cell; it is interesting that the actual diameter of the centre of the receptive field of a ganglion cell is frequently equal to the area over which its dendrites spread; the periphery exerts its effects presumably by means of amacrine cells that are capable of connecting with bipolars over a wide area. These amacrine cells could exert an inhibitory action on the bipolar cells connected to the receptors of the central zone of the field, preventing them from responding to these receptors; in this case, the ganglion cell related to these bipolars would be of an on-centre and off-periphery type.

THE ELECTRORETINOGRAM

If an electrode is placed on the cornea and another, indifferent electrode, placed, for example, in the mouth, illumination of the retina is followed by a succession of electrical changes; the record of these is the electroretinogram, or ERG. Analysis has shown that the electrode on the cornea picks up changes in potential occurring successively at different levels of the retina, so that it is possible to recognize, for example, the electrical changes occurring in the rods and cones—the receptor potentials—those occurring in the horizontal cells, and so on. In general, the electrical changes caused by the different types of cell tend to overlap in time, so that the record in the electroretinogram is only a faint and attenuated index to the actual changes; nevertheless, it has, in the past, been a valuable tool for the analysis of retinal mechanisms. Thus, the most prominent wave—called the b- wave—is closely associated with discharge in the optic nerve, so that in animals, including humans, the height of the b- wave can be used as an objective measure of the response to light. Hence, the sensitivity of the dark-adapted frog's retina to different wavelengths, as indicated by the heights of the b- waves, can be plotted against wavelength to give a typical scotopic sensitivity curve with a maximum at 5000 angstroms (one angstrom = 1×10^{-4} micrometre) corresponding to the maximum for absorption of rhodopsin.

Electrophysiology has been used as a tool for the examination of the basic mechanism of flicker and fusion. The classical studies based on the electroretinogram indicated that the important feature that determines fusion in the cone-dominated retina is the inhibition of the retina caused by each successive light flash, inhibition being indicated by the *a*- wave of the electroretinogram. In the rod-dominated retina—e.g., in humans under scotopic conditions—the *a*- wave is not prominent, and fusion depends simply on the tendency for the excitatory response to a flash to persist, the inhibitory effects of a succeeding stimulus being small. More modern methods of analysis, in which the discharges in single ganglion cells in response to repeated flashes are measured, have defined fairly precisely the nature of fusion, which, so far as the retinal message is concerned, is a condition in which the record from the ganglion cell becomes identical with the record observed in the ganglion cell during spontaneous discharge during constant illumination.

RESOLVING POWER

Although the resolving power of the retina depends on the size and density of packing of the receptors in the retina, it is the neural organization of the receptors that determines whether the brain will be able to make use of this theoretical resolving power. It is therefore of interest to examine the responses of retinal ganglion cells to gratings, either projected as stationary images on to the receptive field or moved slowly across it. One group of investigators showed that ganglion cells of the cat differed in sensitivity to a given grating when the sensitivity was measured by the degree of contrast between the black and white lines of the grating necessary to evoke a measurable response in the ganglion cell. When the lines were made very fine (i.e., the "grating-frequency" was high), a point was reached at which the ganglion cell failed to respond, however great the contrast; this measured the resolving power of the particular cell being investigated. The interesting feature of this work is that individual ganglion cells had a special sensitivity to particular grating-frequencies, as if the ganglion cells were "tuned" to particular frequencies, the frequencies being measured by the number of black and white lines in a given area of retina. When the same technique was applied to human subjects, the electrical changes recorded from the scalp being taken as a measure of the response, the same results were obtained.

COLOUR VISION

The ability to distinguish among various wavelengths of light waves and to perceive the differences as differences in hue defines colour vision. The normal human eye can discriminate among hundreds of such bands of wavelengths as they are received by the colour-sensing cells (cones) of the retina. There are three types of cones, each of which contains a distinctive type of pigment; one cone absorbs longer wavelengths (red light), another middle wavelengths (green light), and the third type shorter wavelengths (blue-violet light). A given colour stimulates all three types of receptors with varying effectiveness, and the pattern of these responses determines the colour perceived. In 1986 researchers identified the genes that correspond to the red, green, and blue pigments.

The spectrum, obtained by refracting light through a prism, shows a number of characteristic regions of colour—red, orange, yellow, green, blue, indigo, and violet. These regions represent large numbers of individual wavelengths; thus, the red extends roughly from 7600 angstrom units to 6500; the yellow from 6300 to 5600; green from 5400 to 5000; blue from 5000 to 4200; and violet from 4200 to 4000. Thus, the limits of the visual spectrum are commonly given as 7600 to 4000 angstroms. In fact, however, the retina is sensitive to ultraviolet light to 3500 angstroms, the failure of the short wavelengths to stimulate vision being due to absorption by the ocular media. Again, if the infrared radiation is strong enough, wavelengths as long as 10,000–10,500 angstroms evoke a sensation of light.

Within the bands of the spectrum, subtle distinctions may be made in hue (hue is the quality of colour that is determined by wavelength). The power of the eye to discriminate light on the basis of its wavelength can be measured by projecting onto the two halves of a screen lights of different wavelengths. When the difference is very small—e.g., five angstroms—no difference can be appreciated. As the difference is increased, a point is reached when the two halves of the screen appear differently coloured. The hue discrimination measured in this way varies with the region of the spectrum examined; thus, in the blue-green and yellow it is as low as 10 angstroms, but in the deep red and violet it may be 100 angstroms or more. Thus, the eye can discriminate several hundreds of different spectral bands, but the capacity is limited. If it is appreciated that there are a large number of nonspectral colours that may be made up by mixing the spectral wavelengths, and by diluting these with white light, the number of different colours that may be distinguished is high.

Defects in colour vision arise from abnormalities in the wavelength discrimination apparatus. This causes an affected individual to see many colours as identical that people with normal colour vision would see as different. About one percent of males are dichromats; they can mix all the colours of the spectrum, as they see them, with only two primaries instead of three. Thus, the protanope (red blind) mixes only blue and green. In contrast, the normal (trichromatic) subject mixes red and green to produce various reds, oranges, yellows, and many greens. An individual who is red blind, however, is unable to distinguish all these hues from each other on the basis of their colour; if the individual distinguishes them, it is because of their different luminosity (brightness). A person who is red blind matches white with a mixture of blue and green and is, in fact, unable to distinguish between white and bluish-green. The deuteranope (green blind) matches all colours with a mixture of red and blue; thus, a person who is green blind sees white as a mixture of red and blue that appears purple to a person with normal vision. An individual who is green blind also is unable to discriminate reds, oranges, yellows, and many greens, so that both types of dichromat are classed as red-green-blind. For a person who is red blind, however, the spectrum is more limited because the individual is unable to appreciate red. The tritanope (blue blind) is rare, constituting only one in 13,000 to 65,000 of the population; because the person is blue blind, his or her colour discrimination is best in the region of red to green, where that of an individual who is red blind or green blind is worse.

Spectral Sensitivity

At extremely low intensities of stimuli, when only rods are stimulated, the retina shows a variable sensitivity to light according to its wavelength, being most sensitive at about 5000 angstroms, the absorption maximum of the rod visual pigment, rhodopsin. In the light-adapted retina one may plot a sensitivity curve, obtained by measuring the relative amounts of light energy of different wavelengths required to produce the same sensation of brightness; the different stimuli appear coloured, but the subject is asked to ignore the colours and match them on the basis of their luminosity (brightness). This is carried out with a special instrument called the flicker-photometer. There is a characteristic shift in the maximum sensitivity from 5000 angstroms for scotopic (night) vision to 5550 angstroms for photopic (day) vision, the so-called Purkinje shift. It has been suggested that the cones have a pigment that shows a maximum of absorption at 5550 angstroms, but the phenomena of colour vision demand that there be three types of cone, with three separate pigments having maximum absorption in the red, green, and blue, so that it is more probable that the photopic luminosity curve is a reflection of the summated behaviour of the three types of cone rather than of one.

The Purkinje shift has an interesting psychophysical correlate; it may be observed, as evening draws on, that the luminosities of different colours of flowers in a garden change; the reds become much darker or black, while the blues become much brighter. This occurs because in this range of luminosities, called mesopic, both rods and cones are responding, and, as the rod responses become more pronounced—i.e., as darkness increases—the rod luminosity scale prevails over that of the cones.

It may be assumed that the sensation of luminosity under any given condition is determined by certain ganglion cells that make connections to all three types of cone and also to rods; at extremely low levels of illumination their responses are determined by the activity aroused in the rods. As the luminance is increased, the ganglion cell is activated by both rods and cones, and so its luminosity curve is governed by both rod and cone activity. Finally, at extremely high luminances, when the rods are "saturated" and ceasing to respond, the luminosity curve is, in effect, compounded of the responses of all three types of cone.

WAVELENGTH DISCRIMINATION

The night visual system, mediated by rods, is unable to discriminate between different wavelengths; thus, a threshold stimulus of light with a wavelength of 4800 angstroms gives a sensation of light that is indistinguishable from that evoked by a wavelength of 5300 angstroms. If the intensities are increased, however, the lights evoke sensations of blue and green, respectively. Rods are unable to mediate wavelength, or colour, discrimination, whereas the cones can because the rods form a homogeneous population, all containing the same photopigment, rhodopsin. Thus, the response of a nerve cell connected with a rod or group of rods will vary with the wavelength of light.

When the response, measured in frequency of discharge in the bipolar or ganglion cell, is plotted against the wavelength of the stimulating light, the curve is essentially similar to the absorption spectrum of rhodopsin when the same amount of energy is in each stimulus; thus, blue-green of 5000 angstroms has the most powerful effect because it is absorbed most efficiently, whereas violet and red have the smallest effects. In this sense, the rods behave as wavelength discriminators. However, there are pairs of wavelengths on each side of the peak to which the same response is obtained; thus, a blue of 4800 angstroms and a yellow of 6000 angstroms give the same discharge. Moreover, if the intensity of the stimulus is varied, a new curve is obtained, and the same response is obtained with a high intensity of violet at 4000 angstroms as with blue at the lower intensity. In general, by varying the intensity of the stimulus of a single wavelength, all types of response may be obtained, so that the brain never receives a message indicating, in a unique fashion, that the retina was stimulated with, say, green light of 5300 angstroms; the same message could be given by blue light of 4800 angstroms, red light of 6500 angstroms, and so on.

Ideally, colour discrimination would require a large number of receptors specifically sensitive to small bands of the spectrum, but the number would have to be extremely large because the capacity for hue discrimination is extremely great. In fact, however, the phenomena of colour mixing suggest that the number of receptors may be limited.

COLOUR MIXING

The fundamental principle of colour mixing was discovered by English physicist and mathematician Sir Isaac Newton when he found that white light separates spatially into its different component colours on passing through a prism. When the same light is passed through another prism, so that the individual bands of the spectrum are superimposed on each other, the sensation becomes one of white light. Thus, the retina, when white light falls on it, is really being exposed to all the wavelengths that make up the spectrum. Because these wavelengths fall simultaneously on the same receptors, the evoked sensation is one of white. If the wavelengths are spread out spatially, they evoke separate sensations, such as red or yellow, according to which receptors receive which bands of wavelengths. In fact, the sensation of white may be evoked by employing much fewer wavelengths than those in the spectrum: namely, by mixing three primary hues—red, green, and blue.

Furthermore, any colour, be it a spectral hue or not, may be matched by a mixture of these three primaries, red, green, and blue, if their relative intensities are varied. Many of the colours of the spectrum can be matched by mixtures of only two of the primary colours, red and green; thus the sensations of red, orange, yellow, and green may be obtained by adding more and more green light to a red one.

Sir Isaac Newton (1642–1727), English scientist and mathematician. Hulton Archive/Getty Images

To one accustomed to mixing pigments, and to mixing a blue pigment, for example, with yellow to obtain green, the statement that red plus green can give yellow or orange, or that blue plus yellow can give white, may sound strange. The mixing of pigments is essentially a subtractive process, however, as opposed to the additive process of throwing differently coloured lights on a white screen. Thus, a blue pigment is blue because it reflects mainly blue (and some green) light and absorbs red and yellow; and a yellow pigment reflects mainly yellow and some green and absorbs blue and red. When blue and yellow pigments are mixed, and white light falls on the mixture, all bands of colour are absorbed except for the green colour band.

YOUNG-HELMHOLTZ THEORY

It was the phenomena of colour mixing that led English physician and physicist Thomas Young in 1802 to postulate that there are three colour receptors, each one especially sensitive to one part of the spectrum; these receptors were thought to convey messages to the brain, and, depending on how strongly they were stimulated by the coloured light, the combined message would be interpreted as that due to the actual colour. The theory was developed by German scientist Hermann von Helmholtz and is called the Young-Helmholtz trichromatic theory.

As expressed in modern terms, the Young-Helmholtz theory postulates that there are three types of cone in the retina, characterized by the presence of one of three different pigments, one absorbing preferentially in the red part of the spectrum, another in the green, and another in the blue. A coloured stimulus—e.g., a yellow light—would stimulate the red and green receptors, but would have little effect on the blue; the combined sensation would be that of yellow, which would be matched by stimulating the eye with red and green lights in correct proportions of relative intensity. A given coloured stimulus would, in general, evoke responses in all three receptors, and it would be the pattern of these responses—e.g., blue strongly, green less strongly, and red weakest—that would determine the quality of the sensation. The intensity of the sensation would be determined by the average frequencies of discharge in the receptors. Thus, increasing the intensity of the stimulus would clearly change the responses in all the receptors, but if they maintained the same pattern, the sensation of hue might remain unaltered and only that of intensity would change; the observer would say that the light was brighter but still bluish green. Thus, the involvement of several receptors reduces the possibility of confusion between stimuli of different intensity but the same wavelength composition; the system is not perfect because the laws of colour mixing show that the eye is incapable of certain types of discrimination, as, for example, between yellow and a mixture of red and green, but as a means of discriminating subtle changes in the environment the eye is a very satisfactory instrument.

The direct proof that the eye does contain three types of cone has been secured. This was done by examining the light emerging from the eye after reflection off the retina; in the dark-adapted eye the light emerging was deficient in blue light because this had been preferentially absorbed by the rhodopsin. In the light-adapted eye, when only cone pigments are absorbing light, the emerging light can be shown to be deficient in red and green light because of the absorption by pigments called erythrolabe and chlorolabe. The light passing through individual cones of the excised human retina can be examined by a microscope device, and it was shown by such examination that cones

were of three different kinds according to their preference for red, green, and blue lights.

NEURON RESPONSE TO COLOUR

If the three types of cones respond differently to light
stimuli, one may expect to find evidence for this difference in type of response by examining the
electrophysiological changes taking place in the retina;
ideally, one should like to place a microelectrode in or on a
cone, then in or on its associated bipolar cell, and so on up
the visual pathway.

In the earliest studies, the optic nerve fibres of the
frog were examined—i.e., the axons of ganglion cells.
The light-adapted retina was stimulated with wavelengths
of light stretching across the spectrum, and the responses
in arbitrarily selected single fibres were examined. The
responses to stimuli of the same energy but different
wavelengths were plotted as frequency of discharge
against wavelength, and the fibres fell into several categories, some giving a so-called dominator response, in which
the fibre responded to all wavelengths and gave a maximum response in the yellow-green at 5600 angstroms.
Other fibres gave responses only over limited ranges of
wavelengths, and their wavelengths of maximum response
tended to be clustered in the red, green, and blue regions.
These became known as modulators. Further study
revealed that the message in the dominator indicated to
the brain the intensity of the stimulus—i.e., it determined the sensation of brightness—whereas the
modulators indicated the spectral composition of
the stimulus, the combined messages in all the modulators resulting in a specific colour sensation. In the
dark-adapted retina, when only rods were being stimulated, the response was of the dominator type, but the

maximum response occurred with a wavelength of 5000 angstroms, the absorption maximum of rhodopsin.

A more careful examination of the responses in single fibres, especially in the fish, which has good colour vision, showed that things were not quite as simple as originally thought because the response of a ganglion cell, when light falls on its receptive field in the retina, is not just a discharge of action potentials that ceases when the light is switched off. This type of response is rare; the most usual ganglion cell or optic nerve fibre has a receptive field organized in a concentric manner, so that a spot of light falling in the central part of the field produces a discharge, while a ring of light falling on the surrounding area has the opposite effect, giving an off-response—i.e., giving a discharge only when the light is switched off. Such a ganglion cell would be called an on-centre-off-periphery unit; others behaved in the opposite way, being off-centre-on-periphery.

When these units are examined with coloured lights, and when care is taken to stimulate the centres and surrounding areas separately, an interesting feature emerges; the centre and surrounding areas usually have opposite, or opponent, responses. Thus, some may be found giving an on-response to red in the centre of the field and an off-response to green in the surrounding area, so that simultaneous stimulation of centre with red and surrounding area with green gives no response, the inhibitory effect of the off-type of response cancelling the excitatory effect of the on-type. With many other units the effects were more complex, the centre giving an on-response to red and an off-response to green, whereas the surrounding area gave an off-response to red and an on-response to green, and vice versa. This opponent organization probably subserves several functions. First, it enables the retina to emphasize differences of colour in adjacent parts of the field, especially when the boundary between them moves, as indeed it is continually doing in normal vision because of the small involuntary movements of the eyes. Second, it is useful in "keeping the retina quiet"; there are about one million optic nerve fibres, and if all these were discharging at once the problem of sorting out their messages, and making meaning of them, would be enormous. Opponence causes diffuse white light falling on many of these chromatic units to have no effect because the inhibitory surrounding area cancels the excitatory centre. When light is coloured, however, the previously inactive units come into activity.

These responses show that by the time the effect of light has passed out of the eye in the optic nerve the message is well colour-coded. Thus all the evidence points to the correctness of the Young-Helmholtz hypothesis with respect to the three-colour basis. The three types of receptor, responding to different regions of the spectrum in specific manners, transmit their effects to bipolar and horizontal cells. The latter neurons have been studied from the point of view of their colour-coding. The potentials recorded from them were called *S*-potentials; these were of two types, which classified them as responding to colour (*C*-units) and luminosity (*L*-units).

The *C*-type of cell gave an opponent type of response, in the sense that the electrical sign varied with the wavelength band, red and green having opponent effects on some cells, and blue and yellow on others. These responses reflect the connections of the horizontal cells to groups of different cones, the blue-yellow type, for example, having connections with blue and red and green cones, while the red-green would have connections only with red and green cones.

CELLS OF THE RECEPTIVE FIELD

The cells at the next stage, the ganglion cells, give a fairly precisely coded set of messages indicating the chromatic (colour) quality and the luminosity (brightness) of the stimulus, organized in such a way, however, as to facilitate the discrimination of contrast. At higher stages—e.g., in the cells of the lateral geniculate body—this emphasis on opponence, or contrast, is maintained and extended; thus, several types of cell have been described that differ in accordance with the organization of their receptive fields from the colour aspect; some were very similar to ganglion cells, whereas others differed in certain respects. Some showed no opponence between colours when centre and periphery were compared, so that if a red light on the periphery caused inhibition, green and blue light would also do so. Others had no centre-periphery organization, the receptive field consisting of only a central spot; different colours had different effects on this spot; and so on.

In the cerebral cortex there is the same type of opponence with many units, but because cortical cells require stimuli of definite shape and often are not activated by simple spot stimuli, early studies carried out before these requirements were known probably failed to elucidate the true chromatic requirements of these high-order neurons. In general, the responses are what might be predicted on the basis of connections made to lateral geniculate neurons having the chromatic responses already known. Thus the final awareness of colour probably depends on the bombardment of certain higher-order cortical neurons by groups of primary cortical neurons, each group sending a different message by virtue of the connections it makes to groups of cones, connections mediated, of course, through the neurons of the retina and lateral geniculate body.

THE PHOTOCHEMICAL PROCESS

For the energy of light to exert its effect it must be absorbed. The action-spectrum for vision (the sensitivity of the eye to light) in the completely dark-adapted eye has a maximum in the region of 5000 angstroms, and this corresponds with the maximum of absorption of light by the pigment, rhodopsin, extracted from the dark-adapted retina. The amount of light energy absorbed by a single rod at the threshold for vision is extremely small—namely, one quantum—and this is quite insufficient to provide the energy required to cause an electrical change in the membrane of the rod that will be propagated from the point of absorption of the light to the rod spherule (which takes part in the synapse between rod and bipolar cell). There must, therefore, be a chemical amplification process taking place within the rod, and the absorption of a quantum must be viewed as the trigger that sets off other changes, which in turn provide the required amount of energy.

RHODOPSIN

Visual purple, or rhodopsin, is a chromoprotein, a protein, opsin, with an attached chromatophore ("pigment-bearing") molecule that gives it its colour—i.e., that allows it to absorb light in the visible part of the spectrum. In the absence of such a chromatophore, the protein would only absorb in the ultraviolet and so would appear colourless to the eye. The chromatophore group was identified as retinal, which is the substance formed by oxidation of vitamin A; on prolonged exposure of the eye to light, retinal can be found, free from the protein opsin, in the retina. When the eye is allowed to remain in the dark, the rhodopsin is regenerated by the joining up of retinal with opsin. Thus one may write:

$$\text{rhodopsin} \rightleftharpoons \text{retinal} + \text{opsin}.$$

The incidence of light on the retina causes the reaction to go to the right (that is, causes rhodopsin to form retinal plus opsin), and this photochemical change causes the sensation of light. The process is reversed by a thermal—i.e., non-photochemical—reaction, so that for any given light intensity a steady state is reached with the regenerative process just keeping pace with the photochemical bleaching. Dark adaptation, or one element in it, is the regenerative process. The change in the rhodopsin molecule that leads to its bleaching—i.e., the splitting off of the retinal molecule—takes place in a succession of steps; and there is reason to believe that the electrical change in the rod that eventually evokes the sensation of light occurs at a stage well before the splitting off of the retinal. One may describe as a transduction process the chemical events that take place between the absorption of light and the electrical event, whatever that may be; the rod behaves as a transducer in that it converts light into electrical or neural energy.

TRANSDUCTION

Immediately after absorption of a quantum, the rhodopsin molecule is changed into a substance called prelumirhodopsin, recognized by its different colour from that of rhodopsin; this product is so highly unstable that at body temperature it is converted, without further absorption of light, into a series of products. These changes may be arrested by cooling the solution to -195 °C (-319 °F), at which temperature prelumirhodopsin remains stable; on warming to -140 °C (-220 °F) prelumirhodopsin becomes lumirhodopsin, with a slightly different colour; on warming further, successive changes are permitted until finally retinal is split off from the opsin to give a yellow solution. The important point to appreciate is that only at this stage is the chromatophore group split off; the earlier products have involved some change in the structure of the chromoprotein, but not so extreme as to break off the retinal. The precise nature of these changes is not yet completely elucidated, but the most fundamental one—namely, that occurring immediately after absorption of the quantum—has been shown to consist in a change in shape of the retinal molecule while it is still attached to opsin.

Thus retinal, like vitamin A, can exist in several forms because of the double bonds in its carbon chain—the so-called *cis-trans* isomerism. In other words, the same group of atoms constituting the retinal molecule can be twisted into a number of different shapes, although the sequence of the atoms is unaltered. While attached to the opsin molecule in the form of rhodopsin, the retinal has a shape called 11-*cis*, being somewhat folded, while on conversion to prelumirhodopsin the retinal has a straighter shape called all-*trans*; the process is called one of photoisomerization, the absorption of light energy causing the molecule to twist into a new shape. Having suffered this alteration in shape, the retinal presumably causes some instability in the opsin, making it, too, change its shape, and thereby exposing to the medium in which it is bathed chemical groupings that were previously shielded by being enveloped in the centre of the molecule. It may be assumed that these changes in shape induce alterations in the light-absorbing character of the molecule that permit the recognition of the new forms of molecule represented by lumirhodopsin, metarhodopsins I and II, and so on.

The final change is more drastic because it involves the complete splitting off of the retinal; an earlier stage—namely, the conversion of metarhodopsin I to metarhodopsin II—has been shown to involve a bodily change in position of the retinal, which in rhodopsin is linked to the lipid (fatty) portion of the molecule, whereas in metarhodopsin II it is found to have become attached to an amino acid in the backbone-chain of the protein (amino acids are subunits of proteins). Thus, in its native unilluminated state, retinal is attached to a lipid, which is presumably linked to the protein, so that rhodopsin is more properly called a chromolipoprotein rather than a chromoprotein. The outer segments of the rods are constituted by membranous disks, and it is well established that the material from which these membranes are constructed is predominantly lipid, so that one may envisage the rhodopsin molecules as being, in fact, part of the membrane structure. The techniques used for extraction presumably tear the molecules from the main body of the lipid, but some of the lipid remains with the protein and retinal to constitute the link holding these two parts together.

Within the retina these chemical changes are all reversible, so that when a steady light is maintained on the retina the latter will contain a mixture of several or all of the intermediate compounds. In the dark, all will be gradually reconverted to rhodopsin. Because lack of vitamin A, from which retinal is derived, causes night blindness, some of the retinal must get lost from the eye to the general circulation; and it is actually replaced by the cells of the pigment epithelium, which are closely associated with the rods.

As to which of these chemical changes acts as the trigger for vision, there is some doubt. The discovery that the transition from metarhodopsin I to metarhodopsin II involves an actual shift of the retinal part of the molecule from linkage to lipid to linkage to protein reinforces the belief that this particular shift is sufficient to lead ultimately to electrical discharges in the optic nerve.

CHAPTER 5

VISION AND THE BRAIN

Vision is a type of sensory perception, and as such the brain plays a crucial role in the interpretation of information transmitted from the retina. There are several areas of the brain that are involved in this process. Information about an object in the visual field travels to the visual centres in the brain in the form of electrical impulses. These impulses, which originate in the cells of the retina, are sent along neuronal tracts that define the visual pathway in the brain.

One example of how the brain interprets visual information is provided by stereoscopy. In binocular vision, each eye forms an image of an object on its retina, and as a result information about two images, in the form of impulses from both retinas, are sent to the optic nerve in the brain and are ultimately received by the visual centres at the back of the brain. There, the impulses from the two views of the same object are unified, resulting in a stereoscopic image. The brain uses information obtained from stereoscopic vision to judge the distance to an object, thereby providing perspective.

THE VISUAL PATHWAY

The axons of the ganglion cells converge on the region of the retina called the papilla or optic disk. They leave the globe as the optic nerve, in which they maintain an orderly arrangement in the sense that fibres from the macular zone of the retina occupy the central portion, the fibres from the temporal half of the retina take up a concentric position, and so on; when outside the orbit, there is a partial decussation (crossover). The fibres from the nasal halves of each retina cross to the opposite side of the brain, while those from the temporal halves remain uncrossed. This partial decussation is called the chiasma. The optic nerves after this point are called the optic tracts, containing nerve fibres from both retinas. The result of the partial decussation is that an object in, say, the right-hand visual field produces effects in the two eyes that are transmitted to the left-hand side of the brain only. With

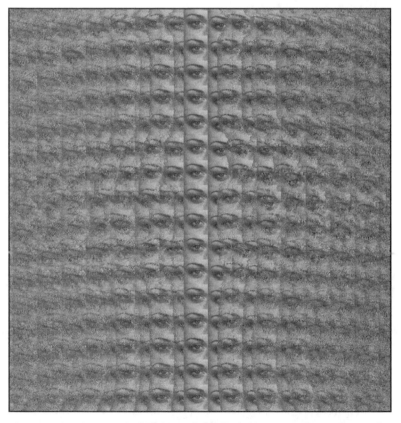

A stereogram is an optical illusion of depth. A viewer can see an image that appears three-dimensional by putting one's nose on the image, focusing the eyes beyond the image on the page, and then moving back. The slight difference in repeated figures creates the illusion of depth in the 2D image, just as the slight difference in perspective between one's eyes creates the perception of depth on 3-D objects and screens. © www.istockphoto.com / Joseph Jean Rolland Dubé

cutaneous (skin) sensation there is a complete crossing-over of the sensory pathway; thus, information from the right half of the body, and the right visual field, is all conveyed to the left-hand part of the brain by the time that it has reached the diencephalon (the posterior part of the forebrain).

FUSION OF RETINAL IMAGES

The crossing over of nerves that is partial decussation serves the needs of frontally directed eyes by permitting binocular vision, which consists in the fusion of the responses of both eyes to a single object. In many lower mammals, with laterally directed eyes and therefore limited binocular vision, the degree of crossing over is much greater, so that in the rat, for example, practically all of the optic nerve fibres pass to the opposite side of the brain.

The fibres of the optic tracts relay their messages to special nerve cells called the lateral geniculate bodies in the diencephalon (the rear portion of the forebrain). Lateral geniculate bodies are a kind of visual relay station. They convey messages to nerve cells in the occipital cortex of the same side. (The occipital cortex is the outer substance in the posterior portion of the brain.)

THE VISUAL FIELD

If one eye is fixed on a point in space, the visual field for this eye may be thought of as the part of a surface of a sphere on to which all visible objects are projected. The limits to this field will be determined both by the capabilities of the retina and the accessibility of light rays from the environment. The field can be measured on a perimeter, a device for ascertaining the point on a given meridian where a white spot just appears or disappears from vision when moved along this meridian. (A meridian is a curve on the surface of a sphere that is formed by the intersection of the sphere surface and a plane passing through the centre of the sphere.) The field is recorded on a chart. On the nasal side, the field is restricted to about 60° from the midline. This is due to the obstruction caused by the nose, since the retina extends nearly as far forward on the temporal side of the globe as on the nasal side. It is customary to refer to the binocular visual field as that common to the two eyes, the uniocular field being the extreme temporal (outside) region peculiar to each eye. The binocular field is determined in the horizontal meridian by the nasal field of each eye, and so will amount to about 60° to either side of the vertical meridian.

LATERAL GENICULATE BODY

The dorsal (posterior) nucleus of the lateral geniculate body, where the optic track fibres relay, has six layers, and the crossed fibres relay in layers 1, 4, and 6, while the uncrossed fibres relay in layers 2, 3, and 5; thus, at this level, the impulses from the two eyes are kept separate, and when the discharges in geniculate neurons are recorded electrically it is rare to find any responding to stimuli in both eyes.

The optic tract fibres make synapses with nerve cells in the respective layers of the lateral geniculate body, and the axons of these third-order nerve cells pass upward to the calcarine fissure (a furrow) in each occipital lobe, a section in the back of the brain. This area is called the striate (striped) area because of bands of white fibres—axons from nerve cells in the retina—that run through it. It is also identified as Brodmann area 17, named after German scientist Korbinian Brodmann, who divided the cerebral cortex into 52 different sections. It is at this level that the impulses from the separate eyes meet at common cortical neurons, or nerve cells, so that when the discharges in single cortical neurons are recorded it is usual to find that they respond to light falling in one or the other eye. It is probable that it is when the retinal messages have reached this level of the central nervous system, and not before, that the human subject becomes aware of the visual stimulus, since destruction of the area causes absolute blindness in humans. Because of the crossing over of partial decussation, however, the removal of only one striate cortex will not cause complete blindness in either eye, since only messages from two halves of the retinas will have been blocked; the same will be true if one optic tract is severed or one lateral geniculate body is destroyed. The result of such lesions will be half-blindness, or hemianopia, the messages from one half of the visual field being obliterated.

Some of the fibres in the optic tracts do not relay in the lateral geniculate bodies but pass instead to a midbrain region—the pretectal centre—where they mediate (transmit) reflex alterations in the size of the pupil. Thus, in bright light, the pupils are constricted; this happens by virtue of the pupillary light reflex mediated by these special nerve fibres. Removal of the occipital cortex, although it causes blindness in the opposite visual field, does not destroy the reaction of the pupils to light; if the optic nerve is cut, however, the eye will be both completely blind and also unreactive to light falling on this eye. The pupil of the blind eye will react to light falling on the other eye by virtue of a decussation in the pupillary reflex pathway.

Because of the ordered manner in which the optic tract fibres relay in the lateral geniculate bodies and from there pass in an orderly fashion to the striate area, when a given point on the retina is stimulated, the response recorded electrically in either the lateral geniculate body or the striate area is localized to a small region characteristic for that particular retinal spot. When the whole retinal field is stimulated in this point-to-point way, and the positions on the geniculate or striate gray matter on which the responses occur are plotted, it is possible to plot on these regions of the brain maps of the retinal fields or, more usually, maps of the visual fields.

Brodmann area 17 is the primary visual centre in the sense that, in primates, all of the geniculate fibres project onto it and none projects onto another region of the cortex. There are two other areas containing neurons that have close connections with the eye; these are the parastriate and peristriate areas, or Brodmann areas 18 and 19, respectively, in close anatomical relationship to one another and to area 17. They are secondary visual areas in the sense that messages are relayed from area 17 to area 18 and from area 18 to area 19, and, because area 17 does not relay to regions beyond area 18, these circumstriate areas are the means whereby visual information is brought into relation with more remote parts of the cortex. Thus in writing, the eyes direct the activities of the fingers, which are controlled by a region of the frontal cortex, so that one may presume that visual information is relayed to this frontal region. In the monkey, bilateral destruction of the areas causes irrecoverable loss of a learned visual discrimination, but this can be relearned after the operation. In humans, lesions in this region are said to cause disturbances in spatial orientation and stereoscopic vision, but much more knowledge is required before specific functions can be attributed to these circumstriate areas, if, indeed, this is possible.

INTEGRATION OF RETINAL INFORMATION

The two halves of the retina, and thus of the visual field, are represented on opposite cerebral hemispheres, but the visual field is perceived as a unity and hence one would expect an intimate connection between the two visual cortical areas.

The great bulk of the connections between the two sides of the cerebral mantle are made by the interhemispheric commissure (the point of union between the two hemispheres of the cerebrum) called the corpus callosum, which is made up of neurons and their axons and dendrites that make synapses with cortical neurons on symmetrically related points of the hemispheres. Thus, electrical stimulation of a point on one hemisphere usually gives rise to a response on a symmetrically related point on the other, by virtue of these callosal connections. The striate area is an exception, however, and it is by virtue of the connections of the striate neurons with the area 18 neurons that this integration occurs, the two areas 18 on opposite hemispheres being linked by the corpus callosum.

Usually stereopsis, or perception of depth, is possible by the use of a single hemisphere because the images of the same object formed by right and left eyes are projected to the same hemisphere; however, if the gaze is fixed on a distant point and a pin is placed in line with this but closer to the observer, a stereoscopic perception of the distant point and the pin can be achieved by the fusion of disparate images of the pin, but the images of the pin actually fall on opposite retinal halves, so that this fusion must be brought about by way of the corpus callosum.

In experimental animals it is possible, by section of the chiasma, to ensure that visual impulses from one eye pass only to one hemisphere. If this is done, an animal trained to respond to a given pattern and permitted to use only one eye during the training is just as efficient, when fully trained, in making the discrimination with the other eye. There has thus been a callosal transfer of the learning so that the hemisphere that was not directly involved in the learning process can react as well as that directly involved. If the corpus callosum is also sectioned, this transfer is impossible, so that the animal, trained with one eye, must be trained again if it is to carry out the task with the other eye only.

The visual pathway so far described is called the geniculostriate pathway, and in humans it may well be the exclusive one from a functional aspect because lesions in this pathway lead to blindness. Nevertheless, many of the optic tract fibres, even in humans, relay in the paired formation on the roof of the midbrain called the superior colliculi. From the colliculi there is no relay to the cortex, so that any responses brought about by this pathway do not involve the cortex. In humans, lesions in the striate area, which would of course leave the collicular centres intact, cause blindness, so that the visual fibres in these centres serve no obvious function. In some animals, removal of the striate areas does not cause complete blindness; in fact, it is often difficult to determine any visual impairment from a study of the behaviour of the animals. Thus, in reptiles and birds, vision is barely affected, so that a pigeon that has been subjected to the operation can fly and avoid obstacles as well as a normal pigeon. In rabbits, removal of the occipital lobes causes some impairment of vision, but the animal can perform such feats as avoiding obstacles when running and recognizing food by sight. In the monkey, the effects are more serious, but the animal can be trained to discriminate lights of different intensity and even the shapes of objects, provided that these are kept in continual motion. It seems likely, then, that it is the visual pathway through the colliculi that permits the use of the eyes in the absence of visual cortex, although the connections of the optic tract fibres with the pulvinar of the thalamus (an area in the diencephalon), established in some animals, may well permit the use of regions of the cortex other than those denoted as visual.

PERCEPTUAL ASPECTS OF VISION

Binocolar vision is a complex phenomenon. Objects are perceived in definite positions in space. These positions are both definite in relation to each other and to the person perceiving them. The first problem, then, is to analyze the physiological basis for this spatial perception.

RELATIVE POSITIONS OF OBJECTS

The perception of the positions of objects in relation to each other is essentially a geometrical problem. For example, in the perception of these relationships by one eye, monocular perception, a group of objects produces images on the retina in a certain fixed geometrical relationship. The neural requirements for this interpretation are (1) that the retina be built up of elements that behave as units throughout their conducting system to the visual cortex, and (2) that the retinal elements have "local signs." The local sign could represent an innate disposition to see things in a particular way. Or, it could result from experience—the association of the direction of objects in space, as determined by such evidence as that provided by touch, with the retinal pattern of stimulation. In neurophysiological terms, the retinal elements are said to be connected to cortical cells, each being specific for a given element, so that when a given cortical cell is excited the awareness is of a specific local sign. Studies of the projection of the retina on the cerebral cortex have confirmed this.

POSITION IN RELATION TO OBSERVER

The recognition of the directions of objects in relation to the observer is more complex. The direction of projection of a retinal point is constantly modified to take into account movements of the eye; this may be called psychological compensation. Correct projection is achieved by projecting the stimulated retinal point through the nodal point of the eye. Movements of the eye caused by movements of the head must be similarly compensated. As a result, any point in space remains fixed in spite of movements of the eye and head. Given this system of compensated projection, the recognition of direction in relation to the individual is feasible. For example, D may be said to be due north or, more vaguely, "over there"; when the head is turned, since D is perceived to be in the same place, it is still due north or "over there." In some circumstances, the human subject makes an error in projecting his or her retinal image, so that the object giving rise to the image appears to be in a different place from its true one; the image is said to be falsely projected. If the eye is moved passively, for example, by pulling on the conjunctiva with forceps, the subject has the impression that objects in the outside world are moving in a direction opposite to that of the eye.

The apparent movement of an afterimage, when the eye moves, is an excellent illustration of psychological compensation. A retinal stimulus, being normally projected through the nodal point, is projected into different points in space as the eye moves; an afterimage can be considered to be the manifestation of a continued retinal impulse, and its projection changes as the eye moves. The afterimage thus appears to move in the same direction as that of the movement of the eye. Whether the drift of an afterimage across the field of view is entirely due to eye movements is difficult to say. One certainly has the impression that the eye is chasing the afterimage.

Visual Estimates: Directions of Lines

So far, consideration has been given to the problem of estimating the positions of points in relation to each other and to the observer. The estimate of the directions of lines involves no really new principles, since, if two points, A and B, are exactly localized, the direction of the line AB can be appreciated. The organization of the neural connections of the retina and higher visual pathway is such as to favour the accurate recognition of direction; for the moment, the question of the maintenance of a frame of reference must be considered, in the sense that a map has vertical and horizontal lines with which to compare other directions. In fact, the vertical and horizontal meridians of the retina seem to be specialized as frames of reference; the accuracy with which a human subject can estimate whether a line is vertical or horizontal is very great.

An important point in this connection is that of the effects of eye movements on interpretation of the directions of lines because, when the eye moves to positions different from the primary straight-ahead position, the images of vertical lines will not necessarily fall on its vertical meridian. This can be due to an actual torsion of the eye about its anteroposterior (fore and aft) axis or to distortion of the retinal image. This means, then, that the line on the retina that corresponds to verticality in one position of the eye does not correspond to verticality in another, so that, once again, the space representation centre must take account not only of the retinal elements that have been stimulated but also of the corollary motor discharge.

VISUAL ESTIMATES: COMPARISON OF LENGTHS

The influence of the movements of the eyes in the estimation of length was emphasized by Helmholtz. An accurate comparison of the lengths of two parallel lines AB and CD can be made, whereas if an attempt is made to compare the nonparallel lines $A'B'$ and $C'D'$, quite large errors occur. According to Helmholtz, the eye fixates first the point A, and the line AB falls along a definite row of receptors, thereby indicating its length. The eye is now moved to fixate C, and if the image of CD falls along the same set of receptors the length of CD is said to be the same as that of AB. Such a movement of the eye is not feasible with lines that are not parallel. Similarly, the parallelism, or otherwise, of pairs of lines can be perceived accurately because on moving the eye over the lines the distance between them must remain the same.

Fairly accurate estimates of relative size may be made, nevertheless, without movements of the eyes. If two equal lines are observed simultaneously, the one with direct fixation and the other with peripheral vision, their images fall, of course, on different parts of the retina; if the images were equally long it could be stated that a certain length of stimulated retina was interpreted as a certain length of line in space. It is probable that this is roughly the basis on which rapid estimates of length depend, although there are such complications as the fact that the retina is curved so that lines of equal length in different parts of the retina do not produce images of equal length on the retina.

Many instances have been cited of well-defined and consistent errors in visual estimates under special conditions. There is probably no single factor by which the errors can be explained, but the tendency for distinctly perceptible differences to appear larger than those more vaguely perceived is important.

DEPTH PERCEPTION

The image of the external world on the retina is essentially flat or two-dimensional, and yet it is possible to appreciate its three-dimensional character with remarkable precision; to a great extent this is by virtue of the simultaneous presentation of different aspects of the world to the two eyes, but even when the subject views the world with a single eye it does not appear flat and he or she can, in fact, make reasonable estimates of the relative positions of objects in all three dimensions. Examples of monocular cues are the apparent movements of objects in relation to each other when the head is moved. Objects nearer the observer move in relation to more distant points in the opposite direction to the movement of the head. Perspective, by which is meant the changed appearance of an object when it is viewed from different angles, is another important clue to depth. Thus the projected retinal image of an object in space may be represented as a series of lines on a plane—e.g., a box—these lines, however, are not a unique representation of the box because the same lines could be used to convey the impression of a perfectly flat object with the lines drawn on it, or of a rectangular, but not cubical, box viewed at a different angle. In order that a three-dimensional object be correctly represented to the subject on a two-dimensional surface, he or she must know what the object is; i.e., it must be familiar. Thus a bicycle is a familiar object. If it is viewed at an angle from the observer the wheels seem elliptical and apparently differ in size. Because the observer knows that the wheels are circular and of the same size, he or she perceives depth in a two-dimensional pattern of lines. The perception of depth in a two-dimensional pattern thus depends greatly on experience—the knowledge of the true shape of things when viewed in a certain way. Other cues are light and shade, overlapping of contours, and relative sizes of familiar objects.

BINOCULAR VISION

The cues to depth are essentially uniocular; they would permit the appreciation of three-dimensional space with a single eye. When two eyes are employed, two additional factors play a role, the one not very important—namely, the act of convergence or divergence of the eyes—and the other very important—namely, the stereoscopic perception of depth by virtue of the dissimilarity of the images presented by a three-dimensional object, or array of objects, to the separate eyes.

When a three-dimensional object or array is examined binocularly, the nearer points or objects require greater convergence for fixation than the more distant points or objects, so that this provides a cue to the three-dimensional character of the presentation. It is by no means a necessary cue, since presentation of the array for such a short time that movements of the eyes cannot occur still permits the three-dimensional perception, which is achieved under these conditions by virtue of the dissimilar images received by the two retinas.

A stereogram contains two drawings of a three-dimensional object taken from different angles, chosen such that the pictures are right- and left-eyed views of the object. When the stereogram is placed in a stereoscope, an optical device for enabling the two separate pictures to be fused and seen single, the impression created is one of a three-dimensional object. The perception is immediate and is not a matter of interpretation. Clearly, with the stereoscope the situation is simulated as it normally occurs.

To appreciate the full implications of the stereoscopic perceptual process, one must examine some simpler aspects of binocular vision.

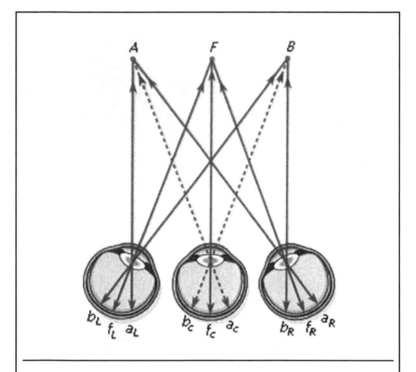

The images of the points F, A, and B on the two retinas are transposed to the retina of a hypothetical eye midway between the two. The pairs of images a_L and a_R, b_L and b_R, and so on, coincide on the cyclopean retina indicating that the stimulated retina points are projected to a common direction (see text).

The cyclopean system of projection. Copyright Encyclopaedia Britannica; rendering for this edition by Rosen Educational Services.

The figure on the previous page illustrates the situation in which a subject is fixating (fixing his gaze on) the point F so that the images of F fall on the foveal (retinal) points fL and fR, respectively. F is seen as a single point because the retinal points fL and fR are projected to the same point in space, and the projection is such that the subject says that the point F is straight in front of him, although it is to the right of his left eye and to the left of his right eye. The two eyes in this case are behaving as a single eye, "the cyclopean eye," situated in the centre of the forehead, and one may represent the projection of the two separate retinal points, fL and fR, as the single projection of the point fC of the cyclopean eye. As will be seen, the cyclopean eye is a useful concept in consideration of certain aspects of stereoscopic vision.

The points fL and fR may be defined as corresponding points because they have the same retinal direction values. The images formed by the points A and B, in the same frontal plane as F, fall on aL and aR and bL and bR; once again the pairs of retinal points are projected to the same points, namely, to A and B, and they are treated as being on the left and right of F, respectively. On the cyclopean projection, they may be said to be localized by the outward projections of aC and bC, respectively.

If a subject is once again fixing the point F, but the point A is now no longer in the same frontal plane as the point F, but closer to the observer, the images of F fall on corresponding points and are projected to a single point in front. The images of A, on aL and aR, do not fall on corresponding points and are, in fact, projected into space in different directions, as indicated by the cyclopean projection. This means that A is seen simultaneously at two different places, a phenomenon called physiological diplopia (double vision), and this in fact does happen, as can be seen by fixing one's gaze on a distant point and

holding a pencil fairly close to the face; with a little practice the two images of the pencil can be distinguished.
Thus, when the eyes are directed into the distance the
objects closer to the observer are seen double, although
one of the double images of any pair is usually suppressed.
Although it is retinal disparity that creates the percept of
three-dimensional space, it is not necessarily the formation of double images, since if the disparity is not large the

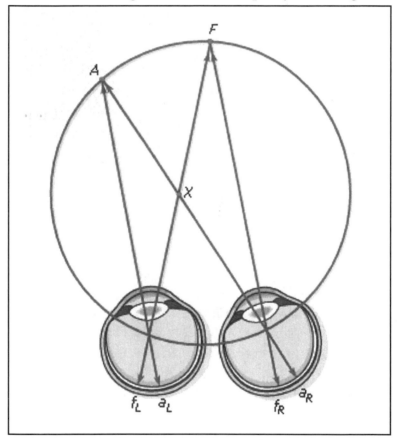

The Vieth-Müller horopter circle. F is the fixation point. If corresponding points are symmetrically distributed about the foveas, the points in space in the fixation plane, whose images fall on the corresponding points, lie on the circle. The images of the point X lie on disparate points (see text). Copyright Encyclopaedia Britannica; rendering for this edition by Rosen Educational Services.

point will be seen single, and this single point will appear to be in a different frontal plane from that containing the fixation point.

To appreciate the nature of this stereoscopic perception one must examine what is meant by corresponding points in a little more detail. In general, it seems that the two retinas are, indeed, organized in such a way that pairs of points are projected innately to the same point in space, and the horopter is defined as the outward projection of these pairs.

One may represent this approximately by a sphere passing through the fixation point, or, if one confines attention to the fixation plane, it may be represented by the so-called Vieth-Müller horopter circle. On this basis, the corresponding points are arranged with strict symmetry, and each pair projects to a single point in space on the horopter circle. Experimentally the horopter turns out to have different shapes according to how close the fixation point is to the observer. The point to appreciate, however, is that the experimentally determined line, be it circular or straight or elliptical, is such that when points are placed on it they all appear to be in the same frontal plane — i.e., there is no stereoscopic perception of depth when one views these points — and one may say that this is because the images of points on the horopter fall on corresponding points of the two retinas.

If the two eyes are viewing an arrow lying in the frontal plane — i.e., with no stereopsis — and to the right the arrow is inclined into the third dimension — i.e., it tends to point toward the observer — all points on the arrow are, in fact, seen single under both conditions. Yet it is clear that there are noncorresponding, or disparate, points on the retinas, which can be projected to a single point. It is essentially this fusion of disparate images by the brain that creates the impression of depth. Furthermore, there is a certain zone of disparity that, if not exceeded, allows fusion of disparate points. This is called Panum's fusional area; it is the area on one retina such that any point in it will fuse with a single point on the other retina.

To return to the stereoscopic perception of three-dimensional space, one may recapitulate that it is because the two eyes receive different images of the same object that the stereoscopic percept happens; when the two images of the object are identical, then, except under very special conditions, the object has no three-dimensionality. A special condition is given by a uniformly illuminated sphere; this is three-dimensional, but the observer would have to use special cues to discriminate this from a flat disk lying in the frontal plane. Such a cue might be the different degree of convergence of the eyes required to fixate the centre from that required to fixate the periphery, or the different degree of accommodation.

Difference in two aspects of the same object (or group of objects) is measured as the instantaneous parallax. The binocular parallax of any point in space is given by the angle subtended at it by the line joining the nodal points of the two eyes; the instantaneous parallax is thus the difference of binocular parallax of the two points considered.

If one places three vertical wires in front of an observer in the frontal plane, one may move the middle one in front of, or behind, the plane containing the other two and ask the subject to say when he or she perceives that it is out of the plane; under correct experimental conditions the only cue will be the difference of binocular parallax, and it is found that the minimum difference is remarkably small, of the order of five seconds of arc, corresponding to a disparity of retinal images far smaller than the diameter of a single cone. With two editions of the same book, it is not possible, by mere inspection, to detect that a given line of print was not printed from the same type as the same line in the other book. If the two lines in question are placed in the stereoscope, it is found that some letters appear to float in space, a stereoscopic impression created by the minute differences in size, shape, and relative position of the letters in the two lines. The stereoscope may thus be used to detect whether a bank note has been forged, whether two coins have been stamped by the same die, and so on.

The stereoscopic appearance obtained by regarding two differently coloured, but otherwise identical, plane pictures with the two eyes separately, is probably due to chromatic differences of magnification. If the left eye, for example, views a plane picture through a red glass and the right eye views the same picture through a blue glass, an illusion of solidity results. Chromatic difference in magnification causes the images on the two retinas to be slightly different in size, so that the images of any point on the picture do not fall on corresponding points; the conditions for a stereoscopic illusion are thus present.

RETINAL RIVALRY

Stereoscopic perception results from the presentation to the two eyes of different images of the same object; if two pictures that cannot possibly be related as two aspects of the same three-dimensional object are presented to the two eyes, single vision may, under some conditions, be obtained, but the phenomenon of retinal rivalry enters. Thus, if the letter *F* occupies one side of a stereogram, and *L* the other, the two letters can be fused by the eyes to give the letter *E*; the letters *F* and *L* cannot, however, by any stretch of the imagination be regarded as left and right aspects of a real object in space, so that the final percept is not three-dimensional, and, moreover, it is not a unitary percept in the sense used in this discussion; great difficulty is experienced in retaining the appearance of the letter E, the two separate images, F and L, tending to float apart. This is a mode of binocular vision that may be more appropriately called simultaneous perception; the two images are seen simultaneously, and it is by superimposition, rather than fusion, that the illusion of the letter E is created. More frequent than superimposition is the situation in which one or the other image is completely suppressed; thus, if the right eye views a vertical black bar and the left eye a horizontal one, the binocular percept is not that of a cross; usually the subject is aware of the vertical bar alone or the horizontal bar alone. Moreover, there is a fairly characteristic rhythm of suppression, or alternation of dominance, as it is called.

Ocular Dominance

Retinal rivalry may be viewed as the competition of the retinal fields for attention; such a notion leads to the concept of ocular dominance — the condition when one retinal image habitually compels attention at the expense of the other. While there seems little doubt that a person may use one eye in preference to the other in acts requiring monocular vision — e.g., in aiming a rifle — it seems doubtful whether, in the normal individual, ocular dominance is really an important factor in the final awareness of the two retinal images.

Where the retinal images overlap, stereoscopic perception is possible and the two fields, in this region, are combined into a single three-dimensional percept. In the extreme temporal fields (i.e., at the outside of the fields of vision), entirely different objects are seen by the two eyes, and the selection of what is to dominate the awareness at any moment depends largely on the interest it arouses; as a result, the complete field of view is filled in and one is not aware of what objects are seen by only one eye. Where the fields overlap, and different objects are seen by the two eyes—e.g., on looking through a window the bars may obscure some objects as seen by one eye but not as seen by the other—the final percept is determined by the need to make something intelligible out of the combined fields. Thus, the left eye may see a chimney pot on a house, while the other eye sees the bar of a window in its place; the final perceptual pattern involves the simultaneous awareness of both the bar and the chimney pot because the retinal images have meaning only if both are present in consciousness.

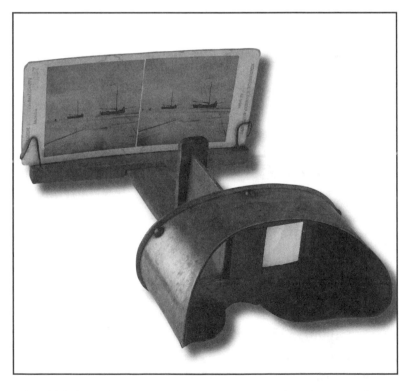

This old-fashioned stereoscope allows viewers to see a three-dimensional image when they look into it. Brand X Pictures/Getty Images

So long as the individual retinal images can be regarded as the visual tokens of an actual arrangement of objects, it is possible to obtain a single percept, and there seems no reason to suppose that the final percept will be greatly influenced by the dominance of one or other eye. When a single percept is impossible, retinal rivalry enters; this is essentially an alternation of awareness of the two fields—the subject apparently makes attempts to find something intelligible in the combined presentation by suppressing first one field and then the other—and certainly it would be incorrect to speak of ocular dominance as an absolute and invariable imposition of a single field on awareness, since this does not occur. Dominance, however, has a well-defined physiological meaning in so far as certain cells of the cerebral cortex may be activated exclusively by one eye, either because the other eye makes no neural connections with it or because the influence of the other eye is dominant.

BINOCULAR BRIGHTNESS SENSATION

When the two eyes are presented with differently illuminated objects or surfaces some interesting phenomena emerge. Thus fusion may give rise to a sensation of lustre. In other instances, rivalry takes place, the one or other picture being suppressed, while in still others the brightness sensation is intermediate between those of the two pictures. This gives rise to the paradox whereby a monocularly viewed white surface appears brighter than when it is viewed binocularly in such a way that one eye views it directly and the other through a dark glass. In this second case the eyes are receiving more light, but because the sensation is determined by both eyes, the result is one that would be obtained were one eye to look at a less luminous surface.

NEURONS OF THE VISUAL CENTRES

To elucidate the functions of the various stages in the visual pathway, one must examine the neurons and the responses to a retinal light-stimulus of the individual neurons at the different stages.

GANGLION CELLS

Ganglion cells have receptive fields that indicate a dual type of connection with the rods and cones, as indicated by the centre-periphery organization. A spot of light falling on receptors in the centre of this field may provoke a discharge in the ganglion cell or its optic nerve fibre; it is called an on-response and consists usually in an increase in the background discharge occurring in darkness. If a spot of light falls on a ring of retina surrounding this central region, the effect is one of inhibition of the background while the light is on, and as soon as it is switched off there is a pronounced discharge, the off-response. Other ganglion cells have been shown to have a directional sensitivity, responding to a moving spot of light only if this moves in a preferred direction and showing inhibition of background discharge if movement is in the null direction.

GENICULATE NEURONS

In general, the lateral geniculate neuron is characterized by an accentuation of the centre-periphery arrangement, so that the two parts of the receptive field tend to cancel each other out completely when stimulated together, by contrast with the ganglion cell in which one or another would predominate. Thus, when the retina is illuminated uniformly there is little response in the geniculate cells because of this cancellation. This represents a useful elaboration of the messages from the retina because, to the animal, uniformity is uninteresting; it is the nonuniformity created by a contour or a moving object that is of interest, and the brain is therefore spared from being bombarded by unnecessary information that would result if every receptor response were transmitted to the brain.

CORTICAL NEURONS

When investigators made records of responses from neurons in area 17 there was an interesting change in the nature of the receptive fields; there was still the organization into excitatory (on) and inhibitory (off) zones, but these were linearly arranged, so that the best stimulus for evoking a response was a line, either white on black or black on white. When this line fell on the retina in a definite direction, and on a definite part of the retina, there was, say, an on-response, while if it fell on adjacent areas there was an off-response. Changing the orientation of the line by as little as 15° could completely abolish the responses. The simplest interpretation of this type of receptive field is based on the connection of the cortical cell with a set of geniculate cells with their receptive fields arranged linearly.

Eye Dominance

Most of these units (i.e., cortical cells plus connections) can be excited by a light stimulus falling on either eye, although there is usually dominance of one eye, in the sense that its response is greater; when both eyes are stimulated together, the effects summate. In general, then, when a large number of units are studied, a certain proportion are fired by one eye alone, others by the opposite eye alone, others by both eyes with dominance of one or other eye, while still others respond only when both eyes are stimulated. It is interesting that when kittens are deprived of the use of one eye from birth for several months, this deprived eye is virtually blind and the distribution of dominance in the cortical neurons is changed dramatically; if the left eye is deprived, the right hemispherical cortical neurons show a marked fall in dominance by the left eye, and an increase by the right eye. Thus, the ability of the eye to make use of cortical neurons is not fully developed at birth.

When an electrode is directed downward into the cortex it picks up responses in individual units at successive depths; units having the same directional sensitivity are arranged in columns so that the receptive fields of successive neurons are similarly oriented. When units were classified on the basis of eye dominance, a similar vertical distribution of units was found, overlapping with those based on directional preference. The columns for eye preference were about one millimetre wide, but those for directional preference were considerably finer. This columnar organization of cortical cells is not peculiar to the visual area.

Of special interest is the behaviour of binocularly driven (stimulated) cortical cells, since their responses provide a clue to the fusion of retinal images. The cortical nerve cell receiving impulses emanating from both retinas must select those parts of the two retinal images that are the images of the same point on an object; second, for stereopsis, the nerve cell must assess the small displacements from exact symmetry that give the binocular parallax. In experiments, maximal response was often obtained only when the stimuli fell on disparate parts of the two retinas; these cortical cells were obviously disparity detectors, in contrast to others that gave maximal response when the stimuli fell on strictly symmetrically related parts of the two retinas—i.e., on corresponding points. When successive units, during penetration of the electrode, were recorded, it was found that those requiring the same degree of disparity for maximal response were arranged in columns, as with direction sensitivity, so that, in effect, all these nerve cells were responding to stimuli in a strip of space at a definite distance from the fixation point.

Complex Neurons

The cortical units (cells), with receptive fields organized on a linear basis, have been called simple units in contrast to complex and hypercomplex units. Four types of complex units have been described; as with the simple units, the orientation of a slit stimulus (that is, a line) is of the utmost importance for obtaining maximal response, but unlike the situation with the simple unit, the position on the retina is unimportant. This type of unit makes abstractions of a higher order, responding to direction of orientation but not to position. It is this type of neuron that would be concerned, for example, with determining the verticality or horizontality of lines in space. Space does not permit a description of the receptive field of a hypercomplex cell, but in general its features could be explained on the basis of connections with complex cells.

CHAPTER 6
DISEASES OF THE OUTER EYE

There are a number of diseases and disorders that affect the outer structures of the human eye. These structures include the orbit, the eyelids, the conjunctiva, and the cornea and sclera. Many diseases tend to affect the blood vessels, muscles, nerve supplies, and other components of the outer eye tissues. In addition, whereas some outer eye diseases such as conjunctivitis are common and are easily treated, others such as tumours of the orbit are quite rare and may not be curable. Some conditions affecting the outer eye also may arise as a result of a preexisting disease or infection.

DISEASES OF THE ORBIT

The orbit is the bony cavity in the skull that houses the globe of the eye (the eyeball), the muscles that move the eye (the extraocular muscles), the lacrimal gland, and the blood vessels and nerves required to supply these structures. The remaining space within the orbit is filled with a fatty pad that acts as a cushion for the eye and allows free movement of the globe. With aging, this pad of fat tends to atrophy so that the globe recedes, causing a more sunken appearance of the eye that is often seen in elderly people.

INFLAMMATION OF THE ORBIT

Since the bone that separates the orbit from the nose and the nasal sinuses is rather thin, infection sometimes spreads from the nasal sinuses into the orbit, causing the orbital tissue to swell and the eye to protrude. This condition, called orbital cellulitis, is serious because of the possibility that the infection may spread into the cranial cavity via the pathways of the cranial nerves that reach the eye through the posterior orbit. Infections can also spread to the cranial cavity by way of the blood vessels that lie within the orbit. Prompt administration of appropriate antibiotics in most cases eliminates such infections. However, surgical drainage of orbital abscesses (pockets of pus surrounded by areas of tissue inflammation) may be required. Sterile (noninfectious) inflammatory conditions such as Graves ophthalmopathy (eye disease caused by thyroid dysfunction) also affect the orbit.

The lacrimal glands, the small glands that secrete the watery component of tears and are located behind the outer part of each upper lid, are rarely inflamed but may become so as a complication of viral infection, such as in mumps or mononucleosis (caused by Epstein-Barr virus). Inflammations of the lacrimal sac are much more common. The lacrimal, or tear, sac lies in a hollow at the inner corner of the eye in the front part of the nasal wall of the orbit; under normal conditions, tears run along the margins of the eyelids toward the nose and are drained through two tiny holes (called puncta) connected by small tubes to the upper part of the lacrimal sac. The lower part of the sac is connected to the nose by the nasolacrimal duct, and infection may ascend this passage from the nose and cause an acute painful swelling at the inner corner of the eye (called dacryocystitis). Blockage of the nasolacrimal duct prevents the passage of tears into the nose and results in a watery eye. Such a blockage, which is often accompanied by chronic inflammation in the lacrimal sac, is usually treated in infancy with a simple massaging technique. However, if the problem persists, a procedure to open or stent the tear passageway can be performed to relieve the obstruction. If this approach also fails, a different operation can be undertaken in which a new opening from the lacrimal sac to the nasal cavity is made.

TUMOURS OF THE ORBIT

Tumours in the orbit are comparatively rare and may arise from within the orbit, as an extension from nearby sinuses, or as a metastasis from a distant tumour. Tumours arising within the orbit include lacrimal gland tumours, lymphoid tumours, vascular tumours, and tumours of the optic nerve, among others. Such tumours may be benign or malignant. Orbital tumours can cause a slow and gradual protrusion or displacement of the eye, which may prevent ocular movements from being coordinated with those of the normal eye. If this occurs, the images of the two eyes, which are normally fused, may separate and give rise to double vision (diplopia).

DISEASES OF THE EYELIDS

BLEPHARITIS

Blepharitis is a common inflammation of the eyelids that is marked by red, scaly, crusting eyelids and a burning, itching, grainy feeling in the eye. The eye itself often has some redness as well. Blepharitis can result from either an infectious or a noninfectious process. Infectious blepharitis is more common in young people; the usual cause is colonization by *Staphylococcus* bacteria along the margins of the eyelids or, less commonly, an infection with herpesvirus that involves the eyelids.

Severe cases of blepharitis can result in ulceration of the eyelid margin or the cornea. Noninfectious blepharitis is most commonly caused by seborrhea, a skin disorder arising from overactivity of the sebaceous glands, or by dysfunction of the meibomian glands, which are oil-secreting glands located along the lid margin behind the eyelashes. The condition is remedied by treating the underlying disorder and by regular cleansing of the eyelid margins with gentle soapy solutions, especially since blepharitis tends to be associated with greasiness of the skin and with dandruff. Long-term treatment is often required. Severe cases of staphylococcal blepharitis can also benefit from topical antibiotic treatments.

The skin of the lids is particularly sensitive to allergic processes. Allergic blepharitis is often seen after exposure to ophthalmic medications, cosmetics, or substances in the environment. Along with the typical symptoms, there may be severe itching and thickening of the eyelid skin.

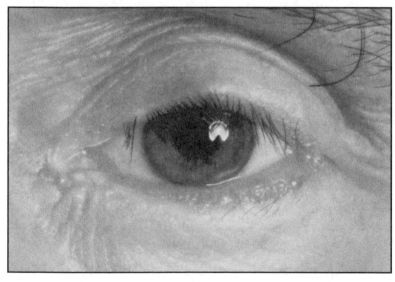

Blepharitis is an inflammation of the eyelids that causes burning and irritation. © CMSP

Treatment involves removing the offending agent and using cool compresses and antiallergy eyedrops.

STY

A sty is an acute, painful, modular infection of one or more glands of the eyelid. Two types are distinguished, the external and the internal sty. The external sty is an infection, usually with *Staphylococcus* bacteria, of a sebaceous gland in the margin of the eyelid. The eye becomes sensitive to light, tears flow copiously, and there is a sensation of a foreign body in the eye. The area of infection is first reddened and then swollen like a pimple or small boil. The breaking of the sty and the discharge of its contents are hastened by application of warm compresses. Sties originating in the lash follicles are usually infectious and start as a painful swelling of the lid. At first it may be difficult to find a localized lesion, but soon one area becomes more swollen, and, as pus forms, a yellow point may be seen near the lid margin.

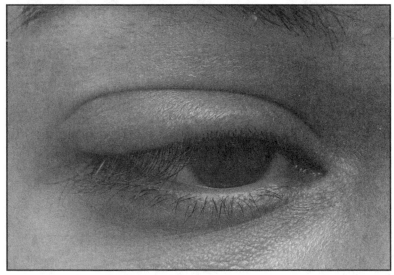

This swollen eyelid reveals a sty. © CMSP

An internal sty results from inflammation of a meibomian gland. It may be caused by an infectious (i.e., staphylococcal) or noninfectious process. Internal sties can be more painful than external sties because they are pressed between the eyeball and the fibrous plate—called the tarsal plate—in the lid. Examination of the internal surface of the lid often shows a red, velvety area with a central yellow spot through which pus may later discharge. Sometimes the meibomian glands suffer from a chronic infection, and a painless firm lump, called a chalazion, appears in the lid and slowly increases in size. The skin can be moved freely over the surface of the lump, showing that the latter is in the deeper tissue of the lid. The inner surface of the lid will show a discoloured area surrounded by inflammation. A chalazion sometimes appears without apparent cause and sometimes as an aftereffect of an internal sty.

Both internal sties and chalazions are treated with warm compresses and massage to try to express their contents. Large, persistent, or particularly bothersome sties and chalazions may require surgical incision and drainage. Often an underlying chronic inflammation or infection of the eyelid margin (such as blepharitis) must be treated in order to prevent recurrence of sties.

SHINGLES

Herpes zoster (shingles) may affect the skin of the eyelids and is of particular importance because the cornea (the transparent covering of the front of the eyeball) and inner eye may also be affected. The condition often starts with pain and redness of the forehead and the eyelids of the same side. Vesicles, or small blisters, form later in the affected area. The pain may be severe, and some constitutional disturbance is common.

MALPOSITION OF THE LIDS

Malposition of the lid is common in elderly people. Although usually not serious in itself, it can give rise to considerable discomfort, irritation, and even impairment of vision. Types of lid malposition include dermatochalasis, ectropion, entropion, and ptosis (or blepharoptosis).

Dermatochalasis

Dermatochalasis is defined as a sagging of the eyelid skin and underlying muscle. It occurs commonly during the aging process. Symptoms may be absent or include brow ache, reduction of superior peripheral vision, sensation of the lid skin resting on the eyelashes, and interference of vision by the eyelashes. Forward displacement of orbital fat may exacerbate this condition. Treatment is predominantly surgical.

Blepharochalasis, a condition distinct from dermatochalasis, is a rare inherited disorder characterized by recurrent episodes of inflammatory lid swelling. This condition typically afflicts young individuals.

Ectropion

Ectropion is the outward turning of the border (or margin) of the eyelid that commonly arises when the lower lid curls away from the globe. The condition most often occurs in elderly persons as a result of age-related relaxation of the eyelid's supporting structures. Other causes include congenital malformation of the lid, paralysis of the muscles that control eyelid movement, excessive scarring and contraction of the eyelid, or mechanical pulling on the eyelid by tumours or improperly fitting eyeglasses. In the lower lid, this may cause the punctum (the opening into the channel that carries tears from the eye into the nasal cavity) to move away from the eyeball. As a result, tears fail to drain properly, and chronic excessive tearing, known as epiphora, is experienced.

Other symptoms of ectropion include eye surface irritation and redness. Chronic exposure of the eye surface from poor lid apposition and altered tear film dynamics can lead to serious corneal problems. Mild cases can be treated with artificial eye lubrication, but definitive treatment is surgical.

Entropion

Entropion is the opposite condition of ectropion, and thus it is defined as an inward turning of the border (or margin) of the eyelid (usually the lower eyelids). It occurs most often in elderly persons. It is commonly caused by age-related alterations in the fibrous and muscular support of the eyelids. The turning in of the lid margin allows the eyelashes to rub against the cornea, with resultant irritation, a condition known as trichiasis. Ulceration of the cornea may be a serious complication. Entropion may also be due to congenital eyelid malformations, spasms of the muscle involved in lid closure (orbicularis oculi), or scarring and contracture from underlying eye disease or trauma. Symptoms from mild cases of entropion can be controlled with artificial eye lubrication and removal of any offending eyelashes. More serious or stubborn cases require surgical correction.

Ptosis

Ptosis, also called blepharoptosis, is a drooping of the upper eyelid. The condition may be congenital or acquired and can cause significant obscuration of vision. In congenital ptosis the muscle that elevates the lid, called the levator palpebrae superioris, is usually absent or imperfectly developed. If severe and not corrected in a timely manner, congenital ptosis can lead to amblyopia and permanent vision loss. Congenital palsy of the third (oculomotor) cranial nerve (which normally stimulates elevation of the upper lid) is a more rare cause of congenital ptosis.

Acquired ptosis has many potential causes, but it is usually due to age-related stretching or displacement of the fibres connecting the levator palpebrae superioris muscle to structures within the upper eyelid. It can also result from muscular diseases (such as muscular dystrophy or myasthenia gravis) or damage to the oculomotor nerve from diabetes, hypertension, atherosclerosis, trauma, or direct compression. In a disorder called Horner syndrome, a slight ptosis occurs in association with a smaller pupil and decreased sweat production on the affected side.

Treatment of persistent blepharoptosis is usually surgical. Depending on the circumstances surrounding the onset of the ptosis, testing may be required to investigate possible underlying causes.

TUMOURS OF THE LIDS

Benign overgrowths of the blood vessels, called hemangiomas, may occur in the lids and give rise to soft, bluish swellings. They are most often present at birth and tend to grow in the first few years of life, sometimes contributing to obscuration of vision and amblyopia. Often they disappear spontaneously, but they can be treated with corticosteroids (steroid hormones such as cortisone, prednisone, or prednisolone), with interferon (potent proteins released by cells of the immune system that block cell reproduction and modulate immune response), or, rarely, by surgical removal. Simple overgrowths of skin, called papillomas, result from viral infections and are common along the lid margin. They require no special treatment except excision or ablation for cosmetic reasons. A nevus (birthmark) is a benign growth, usually pigmented and raised, that arises from pigment cells of the skin. Change in shape, size, or colour of a nevus may indicate transformation into a malignant tumour.

The lids and the skin of the nose near the inner margins of the lids are common sites for the development of skin cancer in older people. The most usual type, called a basal cell carcinoma (or "rodent ulcer"), starts as a small nodule in the skin that gradually enlarges and breaks down to form an ulcer with a hard base and pearly, rolled edges. Bleeding may occur from the base of the ulcer. Although basal cell carcinomas are malignant in the sense that they destroy tissue locally, they do not spread to distant areas of the body by means of the lymph system or the blood vessels. Other malignant cancers affecting the eyelid include sebaceous carcinoma of the eyelid glands and melanoma, the latter of which can arise from preexisting nevi.

DISEASES OF THE CONJUNCTIVA

CONJUNCTIVITIS

Conjunctivitis, also called pinkeye, is an inflammation of the conjunctiva, the delicate mucous membrane that lines the inner surface of the eyelids and covers the front part of the white of the eye. The inflammation may be caused by a viral or bacterial infection. It can also be caused by a chemical burn or mechanical injury, or it may be part of an allergic reaction. Often both the conjunctiva and the cornea are involved, a condition called keratoconjunctivitis. The symptoms of conjunctivitis vary, but they include light sensitivity, redness, itching, a sensation of sand in the eye, and eye discharge (which can be either watery or thick and coloured).

Viral conjunctivitis, caused by viruses that tend to attack the cornea as well as the conjunctiva, occurs more commonly than bacterial conjunctivitis. A variety of viral organisms can give rise to conjunctivitis. Adenoviruses, a group of viruses whose disease-causing members may cause respiratory infections or may survive for long periods in lymphoid tissue (e.g., in the tonsils), may attack the conjunctiva and cornea, causing epidemic keratoconjunctivitis. This condition is highly contagious, frequently spreading from one eye to the other, and is rapidly spread through direct and indirect contact with infected individuals. The onset is acute, with redness, swelling, irritation, and watering of the eye and eyelids, along with a tender swelling of the lymph node in front of the ear. Typically, a person is contagious for at least a week following onset of symptoms. Treatment is mainly supportive, with emphasis on strict hygiene to minimize spread of the virus. The majority of cases resolve without residual problems. Other viruses, such as those that cause cold sores, chickenpox, and measles, also may invade the conjunctiva. Treatment for these cases may include antiviral drops.

Bacterial invasion of the conjunctiva is less common than viral infection. Infection is through direct contact with an infected person or through a person's own nasal or sinus mucosa. Eye discharge is generally thick and coloured, as opposed to the watery discharge of viral conjunctivitis. The organisms most commonly responsible for bacterial conjunctivitis in humans are *Staphylococcus*, *Streptococcus*, and *Haemophilus influenzae* (which may invade the respiratory tract or the brain coverings). Gonococcal conjunctivitis, invasion of the conjunctiva by gonorrhea organisms, was once common among newborn infants, who became infected during delivery. This infection can cause blindness if not treated promptly. It is prevented by routine application of antimicrobials to each eye of an infant after delivery. Gonococcal conjunctivitis can still be transmitted by sexual contact, however, necessitating treatment with systemic and topical medications.

Conjunctivitis frequently results from an allergic reaction to topical eye medications or to airborne allergens such as hay fever pollen. Prominent symptoms include eyelid swelling, itching, eye redness, and a stringy mucoid discharge. Cool compresses and artificial eye lubrication are of benefit, and many antiallergy medications are available. Vernal conjunctivitis is an allergic inflammation that tends to recur in the conjunctivas of susceptible (usually male) children. There are two types of vernal conjunctivitis. In one, the lining of the upper eyelid is affected, with a characteristic red, pebbled appearance. In the second type, the inflammation is manifested by separate yellowish elevations on the conjunctiva near the cornea. Treatment is similar to other cases of allergic conjunctivitis.

A severe form of conjunctivitis that may culminate in blindness occasionally accompanies erythema multiforme, an eruption on the skin and mucous membranes that sometimes occurs in association with a systemic infection or the use of certain medications.

TRACHOMA

Trachoma, although rare in more-developed countries, is a significant cause of preventable blindness in the world. Widespread in some Middle Eastern countries, it has remained common in Asia, India, Central and South America, and Africa and occurs sporadically in southern and eastern Europe. The agent responsible is an intracellular bacterial organism known as *Chlamydia trachomatis*. The disease is contagious and thrives where populations are crowded together in poor hygienic surroundings.

Community health assistants check people for signs of trachoma in a small village in Ethiopia. Trachoma is an eye infection that is the leading preventable cause of blindness in the world. National Eye Institute, National Institutes of Health. STAR Study Team

Shortage of water for washing and the myriads of flies attracted to human waste aid the dissemination of the disease. In some ways trachoma is more of a social problem than a medical problem. When living standards are improved, overcrowding reduced, flies discouraged, and adequate water supplies ensured, the incidence of trachoma decreases rapidly.

The early symptoms of trachoma infection are pain, watering of the eye, and sensitivity to light. At this stage the conjunctival lining of the lids is red and velvety in appearance, and the cornea may show gray areas. Later the conjunctiva appears to have grains of sand embedded in its tissue, and blood vessels grow into the cornea, causing it to thicken and become hazy. Secondary bacterial infections are common, but the real dangers of trachoma lie in the scarring and contracture of tissue that occur when healing takes place. These changes affect the upper lid in particular, causing it to buckle inward in such a way

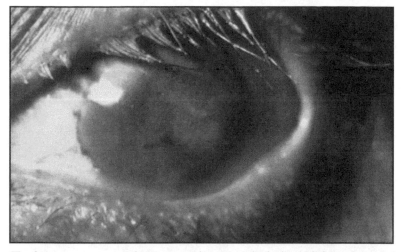

Trachoma can cause trichiasis, a condition in which the eyelid turns inward and eyelashes rub against the eye, resulting in corneal scarring and loss of vision. National Eye Institute, National Institutes of Health. STAR Study Team

that the lashes rub across the already diseased cornea, exacerbating the corneal scarring and potentially leading to blindness. Antibiotic treatment is usually effective at eradicating the infection, although any existing scarring will remain.

PTERYGIUM

A pterygium is an abnormal wing-shaped fold of the conjunctiva that invades the surface of the cornea. Often preceded or accompanied by a pinguecula (yellowish growth in the conjunctiva), pterygia arise from the inner (nasal) or outer (temporal) aspects of the eye. The growth can obscure vision if it encroaches upon the centre of the cornea and thus covers the pupil. Pterygia can contract, altering the shape of the corneal surface and causing astigmatism and blurred vision. Pterygia result from exposure to bright sunlight, wind, and dust, as well as from chronic dryness of the eye. Treatment is surgical removal of the membrane, although recurrence is common in this stubborn affliction.

PINGUECULA

A pinguecula is a very common yellow-white nodule in the conjunctiva, the mucous membrane that lines the eyelid and extends over part of the surface of the eyeball at the front of the eye. Pingueculae are usually found on the side of the cornea near the nose, although it can form on either side of the cornea. Pingueculae occur in elderly persons and are thought to represent degeneration in the conjunctiva as a result of exposure to ultraviolet light. The condition does not usually require medical or surgical treatment, although rare cases of irritation caused by pingueculae can be treated with lubricants.

DISEASES OF THE CORNEA AND SCLERA

The cornea is the clear window of the eye. It covers the iris and pupil and serves as a powerful refractive surface. Any surface irregularity or scar in the substance of the cornea can affect vision. The cornea is an extremely sensitive tissue and contains many nerve fibres that respond to pain. Diseases of the cornea also elicit a flow of tears because of a specialized reflex action that is part of the protective system of the eye.

INFLAMMATION OF THE CORNEA

As with inflammations of the conjunctiva, bacterial infection of the cornea is much less common than viral infection. Of the viruses, the herpesviruses, which cause the common "cold sore" of the lips and skin and the venereal form of herpes, are a frequent cause of corneal ulceration. Infection is most often spread by personal contact. The herpesvirus causes a typical ulcer of the cornea called, from the pattern of the lesion, a dendritic (branching) ulcer. The disease starts with an acutely painful eye, with tearing and sensitivity to light. The ulcer may heal spontaneously or after medical treatment, but the virus often lies dormant in the tissues. Recurrences are common, and with each recurrence there is danger that the virus will extend deeper into the cornea and cause further inflammation and scarring, with eventual vision impairment. Oral antiviral medications or application of antiviral eye drops to the cornea usually cause the ulcer to heal more rapidly. The action of these drugs limits the multiplication of the virus by interfering with the formation of virus deoxyribonucleic acid (DNA) in the host cell.

Bacterial infections of the cornea usually occur after injury to, or breakdown of, the corneal surface, as few bacteria have the power to penetrate the intact surface layers of the cornea. Such ulcers may be extremely severe, and there is always a danger of perforation of the eye, particularly in debilitated patients.

Spores of fungi are present in the atmosphere, and the normal cornea is resistant to infection by these organisms. However, a fungal infection of the cornea can develop after a corneal injury or other lesion, particularly if corticosteroid drugs have been used in the treatment of these conditions. Intensive treatment with antifungal drugs is usually effective in killing the organisms, but a dense scar may be left.

A corneal inflammation may start in the deeper layers of the tissue, either by direct infection or from immune-related processes. One type is seen in adolescents who have congenital syphilis. Both eyes are usually attacked, although there may be an interval before the second eye is affected. As a result of inflammation, the cornea rapidly becomes hazy, and blood vessels grow in from the surrounding tissues to form a pink patch. With the decline in congenital syphilis in developed countries, the condition is becoming increasingly rare.

KERATITIS

Keratitis is a type of inflammation of the cornea. There are several varieties of keratitis, which can be caused by either infectious or noninfectious processes. In many cases, however, changes in the cornea induced by noninfectious keratitis predispose it to secondary infections. Often there is inflammation of both the cornea and the conjunctiva, the mucous membrane that lines the inside of the eyelid and covers the white of the eye (the sclera). In this case, the condition is called keratoconjunctivitis.

Infectious causes of keratitis include bacteria, viruses, fungi, and protozoans. Symptoms vary but may include redness, pain, decreased vision, light sensitivity, discharge, or a frank opacity within the cornea. Treatment often requires culturing the infected corneal tissue and discharge in order to identify the causative organism so as to tailor antimicrobial therapy appropriately. The concurrent use of contact lenses increases the likelihood of serious infection in these cases and raises special considerations for the eye care specialist.

Interstitial keratitis, an inflammation deep in the cornea, may be caused by congenital syphilis, tuberculosis, herpesvirus infection, or even physical injury to the eye. Affected persons may note that their eyes are painful, tend to water, and are sensitive to light. Treatment is directed at eliminating the underlying disease. As with any keratitis, if corticosteroids are used in the course of treatment, close follow-up with an ophthalmologist is required, since certain conditions can worsen with these medications.

In dendritic keratitis, or dendritic ulcer, the cornea is inflamed by infection with the herpes simplex (cold sore) virus or herpes zoster (shingles) virus. The lesions, as the name suggests, follow branching lines, along which minute blisters may form and break, leaving raw areas. The cornea may ultimately become insensitive, so the process may not be painful.

One type of noninfectious keratitis, called keratoconjunctivitis sicca, results from excessive dryness of the cornea. This condition is characterized by dryness and inflammation of the cornea and conjunctiva due to failure to secrete sufficient tears, which in turn can stem from immune disorders or diseases that infiltrate the lacrimal, or tear, gland. The condition is called Sjögren syndrome when the dry eye is associated with certain systemic disorders. In exposure keratitis the cornea may also become dry and inflamed when, because of protrusion of the eyeball or paralysis of the muscle that closes the lids, a person is unable to shut his or her eyes completely. Initial treatment employs aggressive eye lubrication; however, if this fails, closure of the eyelid puncta (tear drainage holes) or surgery to partially close the lids may be needed.

Keratitis can cause the spread of blood vessels onto and into the cornea and can cause visual loss by opacifying the cornea (making it cloudy). Keratitis from chemical burns, particularly burns from acids and alkalis, is a leading culprit. Early flooding of the eye with water, either slightly salted or straight from the tap, is standard procedure, since the extent of the damage depends in large part upon the length of time that the chemical remains in the eye. The most serious chemical burns are caused by alkali, which, if not quickly removed, can do severe and progressive damage to the point of "melting" the cornea.

Rosacea keratitis is a complication of acne rosacea, a disease in which the skin of the face is affected first by pronounced flushing and later by the formation of nodules and pustules. The keratitis may cause severe pain and corneal scarring with impairment of vision. Patients with rosacea keratitis have unusually high levels and abnormal forms of an antimicrobial protein called cathelicidin, which is synthesized by cells of the immune system, such as macrophages and neutrophils. Cathelicidin stimulates the production of inflammatory molecules that contribute to the symptoms and complications associated with rosacea.

Neuroparalytic keratitis is inflammation of the cornea as a sequel to interruption of sensory impulses over the fifth (trigeminal) cranial nerve. The cornea's loss of sensitivity leaves it much more subject to injury, exposure, and infection. This type of keratitis tends to lead to ulceration of the cornea and impairment of vision and may result in perforation of the eyeball, which could necessitate enucleation (removal of the eye). Treatment includes the intensive use of eye lubricants and may also include antibiotics if a secondary infection of the cornea is present.

Other possible causes of keratitis are numerous and include reactions to topical eye medications, toxin exposure, infection and inflammation of the eyelid margins (blepharitis), and various allergic conditions.

SCLERITIS

The sclera is the fibrous covering of the eye that shows up as a dense white layer beneath the transparent conjunctiva. A relatively mild nodular inflammation, called episcleritis, sometimes occurs in the superficial layers just above the sclera. It occurs more often in young and middle-aged adults and usually improves without treatment. In more severe cases, treatment with anti-inflammatory medication may be necessary.

Inflammation of the deeper sclera, called scleritis, is more severe and is often painful.

Scleritis is immune-mediated and is commonly associated with underlying systemic infections, such as shingles (herpes zoster), syphilis, and tuberculosis, or with autoimmune diseases, such as rheumatoid arthritis and systemic lupus erythematosus. Scleritis generally occurs in people in their fourth to sixth decades of life, affects women more often than men, and frequently affects both eyes. It usually produces a severe, deep ocular pain and a localized or diffuse reddish purple discoloration of the sclera. On occasion, scleritis can be severe enough to destroy areas of the sclera and pose a significant threat to the health and visual function of the eye. Other eye complications of scleritis include uveitis, cataracts, keratitis, and glaucoma. Scleritis can also be a harbinger of serious, life-threatening systemic illness. Treatment ranges from topical corticosteroid eye drops to oral nonsteroidal anti-inflammatory agents. Treatment of underlying systemic disease, such as with immunosuppressive medication, may also be a critical component of overall therapy.

Episcleritis, in contrast to scleritis, is typically a benign, self-limited inflammation of the tissues immediately covering the sclera. It produces redness of the eye with or without mild tenderness. Only in rare cases do patients have any associated underlying disease. Treatment is often not necessary but could include topical nonsteroidal anti-inflammatory medications.

Degeneration of the Cornea and Sclera

There are numerous types of corneal degeneration, many of which are rare and some of which are familial. The most common type is keratoconus, a curious condition in which the central part of the cornea, normally spherical in shape, begins to bulge and protrude forward as a cone. The only symptom is deterioration of vision due to irregular astigmatism caused by the changing corneal curvature. Contact lenses are often more effective than eyeglasses in treating this condition. Advanced cases of keratoconus, and most other types of corneal degeneration, may require corneal transplants.

CHAPTER 7
DISEASES OF THE INNER EYE

D iseases and disorders of the inner eye can affect structures fundamental to the visual process. These structures include the uveal tract, the lens, the retina, and the optic nerve. Although diseases such as uveitis, an inflammatory condition of the uvea, may affect people at any age, conditions such as cataracts and glaucoma are frequently associated with aging and occur most often in people over age 65. In addition, there are several inner eye diseases, including congenital coloboma, congenital cataracts, and retinopathy of prematurity, that affect very young infants. Similar to diseases occurring in the structures of the outer eye, some diseases of the inner eye are easily identified and treated, whereas others are only beginning to be understood and are difficult to treat.

UVEITIS

Uveitis is the inflammation of the uvea (or uveal tract), the middle layer of tissue surrounding the eye that consists of the iris, ciliary body, and choroid. Uveitis can affect people at any age, but onset usually occurs in the third and fourth decades of life.

ANATOMICAL FORMS OF UVEITIS

Uveitis is classified anatomically as anterior, intermediate, posterior, or diffuse. Anterior uveitis typically refers to inflammation of the iris and anterior chamber; intermediate uveitis refers to inflammation of the ciliary body and vitreous humour (the jellylike filling in the anterior portion of the eye); and posterior uveitis refers to inflammation of the retina, choroid, or the optic disk (where the optic nerve enters the retina). Diffuse uveitis (panuveitis) implies inflammation of the entire uveal tract.

Most cases of uveitis are idiopathic, meaning the cause cannot be determined. However, when cause can be determined, uveitis is often found to originate from an infection (viral, fungal, bacterial, or parasitic), systemic disease (typically an autoimmune disorder), or injury to the eye. When identified, the most common cause of anterior uveitis is trauma, followed by chronic joint diseases (spondyloarthropathies), juvenile idiopathic arthritis (also known as juvenile rheumatoid arthritis), and herpesvirus infection. Causes of intermediate uveitis may include multiple sclerosis, tuberculosis, syphilis, Lyme disease, or sarcoidosis (a systemic disease characterized by the formation of grainy lumps in tissues). The most common cause of posterior uveitis is toxoplasmosis (a parasitic infection), although in immunocompromised patients it is more likely caused by infection with cytomegalovirus, *Candida*, or herpesvirus. Posterior uveitis can also be caused by ocular histoplasmosis (a fungal infection), syphilis, or sarcoidosis. In rare cases uveitis can be caused by certain drugs, including sulfonamides, bisphosphonates (e.g., pamidronate), or antimicrobials (e.g., rifabutin and cidofovir).

DIAGNOSIS AND TREATMENT OF UVEITIS

The symptoms of uveitis may be subtle but can develop rapidly and vary, depending on the site and severity of inflammation. They can include eye redness, eye pain, blurred vision, light sensitivity, floating spots, and decreased vision. Diagnosis is made on the basis of the clinical findings. Clinical signs of uveitis include dilated ciliary vessels, cells in the aqueous humour, keratin precipitates on the posterior surface of the cornea, adhesion of the iris to the cornea (posterior synechiae), and inflammatory cells in the vitreous cavity (vitritis), sometimes with snowballs (condensations of inflammatory cells) or snowbanking (deposition of inflammatory material in the area where the iris and sclera touch). Other signs may include yellow-white lesions in the retina (retinitis) or underlying choroid (choroiditis), retinal detachment, inflammation of retinal blood vessels (vasculitis), and swelling of the optic disk. Diagnosis is often confirmed with laboratory tests in order to rule out malignant conditions with similar symptoms, such as retinoblastoma, intraocular leukemia, or intraocular lymphoma.

Treatment depends on cause but typically includes topical or systemic corticosteroids and pupil-dilating drugs that relieve pain caused by spasms of the pupil-constriction muscle. However, long-term use of corticosteroids can have harmful side effects, which may include increased blood pressure, renal damage, and osteoporosis. In patients with severe uveitis that is unresponsive to corticosteroids or in patients with complications associated with steroidal therapy, other types of immunosuppressant agents can be used. For example, medications that target specific mediators of the immune response have proved effective in the treatment of uveitis. In particular, molecules that block proteins known as tumour necrosis factor-alpha and interleukin-2 receptor have been shown to modulate immune response in uveitis patients. In addition, the use of intraocular pharmacotherapy via intravitreal injection and surgical implants also can be effective; however, side effects, such as cataract formation and elevated intraocular pressure, are common. Infectious causes of uveitis require antimicrobial therapy. In some cases, vitrectomy, surgical removal of the jellylike material, or vitreous, that fills the interior of the eye cavity, may be necessary.

Patients with suspected uveitis should be examined by an eye doctor within 24 hours; if left untreated, uveitis may permanently damage vision. Uveitis may give rise to other eye conditions, such as cataracts (clouding of the lens or cornea) and elevated intraocular pressure, secondary to inflammation or topical corticosteroid use. Other complications, in addition to increased risk of retinal detachment and adhesions between the iris and lens, include the formation of blood vessels in the iris, retina, or optic nerve and the formation of fluid-filled cystlike swellings on the retina, which can damage vision.

TUMOURS OF THE UVEAL TRACT

Pigmented tumours are the most common tumours arising from the uveal tract. They may be benign (such as a nevus or a mole) or malignant (such as melanoma). The choroid is a common site for these lesions, which can push the retina forward and possibly cause a retinal detachment. Disturbances of vision are the most common symptom, but, if the tumour is neglected, choroidal melanomas may enlarge and cause inflammation and raised pressure within the eye. Small portions of the tumour can enter the bloodstream and settle in distant organs, particularly the liver. The growth of these secondary deposits is often slow, and they may not be apparent until many years after the diagnosis of the tumour in the eye. Treatment options for melanoma vary and include local radiation treatment or removal of the eye (called enucleation).

DISEASES OF THE LENS

The lens is a transparent, avascular organ surrounded by an elastic capsule. It lies behind the pupil and is suspended from the ciliary body by a series of fine ligaments called zonular fibres. Its transparency is the result of the regular arrangement of the internal lens fibres, which form continuously throughout life. Interference with the growth or maintenance of lens fibres can result in the formation of abnormal fibres or fibre arrangements that cannot transmit light as well as the normal lens fibres. An opacity is thus seen in the lens. Minor irregularities are common in otherwise perfectly normal eyes. If the opacity is severe enough to affect vision, it is called a cataract.

Congenital lens opacities of many varieties have been recognized and described since the early days of ophthalmology, but they remained curiosities until the work of an Australian ophthalmologist, Norman M. Gregg, threw new light on their cause—and, indeed, on that of many other congenital defects. In 1941 Gregg noticed that, after an epidemic of German measles (rubella), many of the children whose mothers had contracted the disease in the first two months of pregnancy were born with cataracts, sometimes associated with deafness and congenital heart disease. Congenital cataracts can also be inherited; can be associated with genetic, metabolic, or other infectious diseases and disorders; or may have no known cause or association. Cataracts are one of the primary diseases affecting the lens of the human eye.

CATARACTS

Cataracts cause opacity of the crystalline lens of the eye. They occur in 50 percent of people between ages 65 and 74 and in 70 percent of people over age 75. Typical age-related cataracts can cause cloudy vision, glare, colour vision problems, changes in eyeglass prescription, and, rarely, double vision (only in the affected eye). Usually, these types of cataracts are bilateral, although one eye may be more affected than the other.

Cataracts in the adult may be the result of injury to the lens by a perforating wound, exposure to radiation such as X-rays, chronic inflammation such as uveitis, or ingestion of toxic substances or even of some drugs. The most common form of cataract is age-related cataract, so called because it becomes progressively more common with advancing age. The three common types of age-related cataracts are nuclear sclerotic cataracts, cortical cataracts, and posterior subcapsular cataracts. These cataracts can exist in isolation or in any combination with each other, and each can cause a wide spectrum of vision problems, from unnoticeable to blinding. Nuclear cataracts cause a slow, progressive yellowing or browning of the central core of the lens as it undergoes compression and hardening. Cortical cataracts are spokelike opacities that extend from the lens periphery toward the centre. Advanced cortical cataracts can cause the lens to appear white, a so-called mature cataract. Posterior subcapsular cataracts are located near the very back of the lens and, if present in a troublesome location, can cause vision difficulties even at a relatively small size. In contrast to nuclear or cortical cataracts, posterior subcapsular cataracts tend to occur in younger people and can result from steroid use, exposure to radiation, or trauma. In addition to age-related lens changes, some systemic diseases can promote cataract formation, most notably diabetes mellitus. Management of symptomatic cataracts is surgical, requiring removal of the offending lens and placement of an artificial lens within the eye, if possible.

Cataracts present at birth are termed congenital cataracts, whereas those that are evident within the first year of life are called infantile cataracts. They can affect one or both eyes and can produce severe visual impairment and amblyopia. They can occur by themselves; in association with genetic and metabolic diseases, in utero maternal infections, or toxin exposure; or in combination with other congenital eye problems. Treatment involves surgical removal of the cataractous lens if it interferes with vision. However, placement of an artificial lens within the eye requires special considerations and may not be appropriate, depending on the child's age. Eyeglasses or contact lenses are commonly used postoperatively to improve vision, and occlusion patching of the unaffected eye is often necessary to treat associated amblyopia.

In the early stages of cataract development, some visual improvement can usually be obtained with eyeglasses, but, as the cataract progresses, the visual deterioration becomes sufficiently severe to warrant

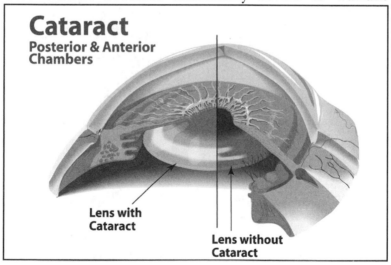

Cataracts cause clouding of the lens of an eye, inhibiting vision.
© M. Eaton/CMSP

surgical treatment. Cataract surgery involves removing the cloudy lens and, in most cases, placement of an artificial lens within the eye.

Lens Dislocation

Lens dislocation occurs when the lens assumes an abnormal position within the eye. The dislocation, which may be congenital, developmental, or acquired (typically via trauma), is usually caused by abnormalities of or injury to a portion of the zonular fibres that anchor the lens to the ciliary muscle. Problems associated with lens dislocation include monocular double vision, decreased vision, and astigmatism.

Lens dislocation is a feature of a number of congenital and hereditary disorders, including Marfan syndrome and Ehlers-Danlos syndrome. Marfan syndrome is associated with cardiac and skeletal abnormalities, whereas Ehlers-Danlos is a condition marked by great elasticity of the skin and double-jointedness. The usual management of the lens dislocation is improvement of vision by means of eyeglasses or rigid contact lenses, although surgical lens removal may eventually be necessary.

DISEASES OF THE RETINA

Detached Retina

Retinal detachment occurs when the retina becomes separated from the underlying layer of supporting cells known as the retinal pigment epithelium. Most commonly, retinal detachments are caused by the passage of fluid through a break, or tear, in the retina, a situation called rhegmatogenous retinal detachment. The fluid is derived from the

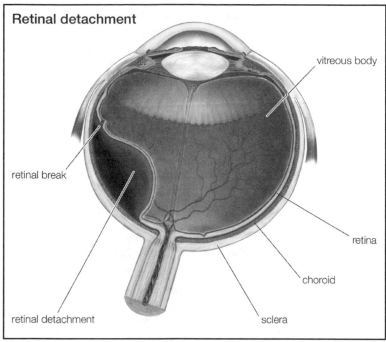

Retinal detachment. Encyclopædia Britannica, Inc.

aging vitreous gel that fills the central eyeball space. The retinal break can result from a number of different mechanisms, including trauma or degenerative changes in the peripheral retina.

Most retinal breaks or tears, however, are the result of the natural changes of the vitreous gel that are often experienced with aging. The vitreous gel is physically attached to the retina, but, if the gel pulls away, the gel's surface usually releases its hold, creating a benign posterior vitreal detachment without a retinal tear. If, however, a portion of the retina is torn during this process, the likelihood that a retinal detachment will soon follow is high. Unfortunately, the symptoms of a benign posterior vitreous detachment and a serious retinal tear are similar. These symptoms include the onset of many "floaters" (deposits in the eye that cause visual spots or shadows), as well as brief, flashing lights in the affected eye. The presence of bleeding within the eye under these circumstances greatly increases the chances that there is a retinal tear. Concern for subsequent retinal detachment is heightened if there is a perception of a gray or black curtain, or veil, being drawn across the eye's visual field.

Not all retinal breaks need treatment, but those that do (especially those associated with a retinal detachment) are often treated with laser, freezing, or a variety of surgical interventions. Failure to reattach the retina in a timely manner can lead to permanent vision loss. Retinal detachment repair is considered more urgent if the centre of the retina (the macula) is still attached, since progression of the detachment to include the macula significantly decreases the prognosis for good postoperative vision. Other types of retinal detachments include tractional detachments, which are caused by abnormal membranes that contract on the surface of the retina (as can occur with advanced diabetic eye disease), and exudative detachments, in which the fluid that leaks under the retina comes from within or beneath the retina.

MACULAR DEGENERATION

Macular degeneration refers to any of several blinding disorders that are characterized by the gradual deterioration of the retina. The central region of the retina contains the macula lutea, which receives focused incoming light and is responsible for providing acute vision. The loss of neurons in the macula causes decreased sensitivity in the centre of the visual field; peripheral vision is usually retained.

Age-Related Macular Degeneration
The most common form of macular degeneration is age-related macular degeneration (ARMD), and the incidence

of this disease increases dramatically with age, affecting approximately 14 percent of those over age 80. AMD is the most common cause of vision loss in the industrialized world and is most prevalent in populations of European descent. In the United States AMD accounts for about 54 percent of vision loss in the non-Hispanic white population, about 4 percent of vision loss in the African American population, and about 14 percent of vision loss in the Hispanic population. In addition, vision loss from AMD is more prevalent in females. The cause of AMD is unknown, but in addition to ethnic origin and gender, several other risk factors have been identified. These include smoking and the inheritance of certain genetic variants, such as those occurring in the genes *CFH* (complement factor H), *APOE* (apolipoprotein E), and possibly *ARMS2* (age-related maculopathy susceptibility).

The diagnosis of AMD is determined by the presence, number, and size of drusen (small masses of extracellular material) under the retina. As the disease progresses, loss of the retinal cells can be seen on clinical exams. Advanced AMD has two forms, often referred to as wet and dry. Wet AMD occurs when new blood vessels sprout from the choriocapillaris (vascular layer in the choroid, the tissue separating the sclera and retina), and dry AMD is the atrophic loss of cells in the macula. Wet AMD can be treated to retard the growth of new blood vessels, which slows vision loss. There is no treatment for dry AMD. The progression of AMD in those at greatest risk of losing vision can be slowed with high-dose dietary supplementation of vitamins C and E, beta-carotene, and zinc, all of which are thought to have an antioxidant function.

Other Forms of Macular Degeneration
Macular degeneration has five known genetic forms for which the causative genes have been identified. Best

disease is a form of macular degeneration that is typically characterized by early onset and is caused by mutations in a gene known as *BEST1* (bestrophin 1). Stargardt macular dystrophy, which is the most common genetic form of macular degeneration, is the only form inherited in an autosomal recessive manner (disease occurs only when mutations are inherited from both parents). It is caused by mutations in a gene called *ABCA4* (ATP-binding cassette, subfamily A, member 4). Stargardt-like macular dystrophy differs from Stargardt macular dystrophy in that it is caused by mutations in a gene called *ELOVL4* (elongation of very-long-chain fatty acids-like 4). Malattia Leventinese (Doyne honeycomb) retinal dystrophy, which is characterized by a honeycomb-like pattern of drusen formation under the retina, is caused by mutations in the gene *EFEMP1* (EGF-containing fibulin-like extracellular matrix protein 1). Sorsby fundus dystrophy, which is clinically similar to wet AMD, is caused by mutations in a gene known as *TIMP3* (tissue-inhibitor of metalloproteinase 3). These forms of macular degeneration, with the exception of Stargardt macular dystrophy, are inherited as autosomal dominant traits; disease occurs when a mutant gene is inherited from one parent. All five of these genetic forms of macular degeneration are rare, occurring in less than 1 in 2,000 people, and can present clinically in children, young adults, and adults.

RETINOPATHY OF PREMATURITY

Retinopathy of prematurity is a disease in which retinal blood vessels develop abnormally in the eyes of premature infants. In mild forms of retinopathy of prematurity, developing blood vessels within the retina, which originate at the optic disk, stop growing toward the periphery of the retina for a period of time. Thereafter, the vessels

This photo shows what someone with normal vision might see if looking at these two boys. National Eye Institute, National Institutes of Health

This photo shows how someone with macular degeneration may view the same scene. National Eye Institute, National Institutes of Health

usually resume their development without deleterious consequences. However, in severe forms of the disease, the stalled blood vessels break through to the surface of the retina and proliferate extensively. These fragile tangles of blood vessels can break, bleed, scar, and pull on the underlying retina, causing complex retinal detachments and blindness.

The likelihood of developing retinopathy of prematurity increases with lower birth weights and earlier deliveries. Retinopathy of prematurity is associated with the administration of high concentrations of oxygen, given to susceptible infants in an attempt to prevent respiratory disease. Despite the potential risk of retinopathy of prematurity, many infants require the use of supplemental oxygen to prevent neurologic dysfunction and loss of life. With current approaches to oxygen therapy and close monitoring, retinopathy of prematurity has become less common. Even so, the disease remains a significant cause of early childhood-onset visual loss, occasionally occurring even in infants who do not receive supplemental oxygen.

When necessary, treatment is aimed at destroying those areas of retina that do not have mature retinal blood vessels, usually with laser therapy or cryotherapy (freezing therapy). Additional complications of retinopathy of prematurity include amblyopia, cataracts, glaucoma, and nearsightedness (myopia), among others.

COLOBOMA

The failure of one or more structures in the eye to fuse during embryonic life, creating a congenital fissure in that eye, is known as coloboma. Frequently several structures are fissured: the choroid, the retina, the ciliary body, and the iris. The fissure may extend to the head of the optic nerve. Colobomata may also be confined to individual structures of the eye. Fissures in the retina cause blind spots (scotomata), and a coloboma in the optic nerve also seriously affects vision.

DISEASES OF THE OPTIC NERVE

The optic nerve, which carries about one million nerve fibres, leaves the globe from the back of the eye and passes through the apex of the orbit into the cranial cavity. It is surrounded by an extension of the membranes that surround the brain. This connection with the intracranial cavity is important because some intracranial diseases cause increased pressure within the skull. Increased pressure is transmitted along the covering of the optic nerve, causing swelling of the optic nerve head, a condition that is visible inside the eye. This swelling of the nerve head of each eye (called papilledema) is one of the most important signs of increased intracranial pressure. If the swelling persists, damage to the fibres of the optic nerve can take place, with subsequent loss of vision.

Optic nerve damage or atrophy may result from optic neuritis, glaucoma, or any serious disease of the retina in which a large amount of neural tissue has been destroyed. It may also follow damage to the optic nerve within the skull or the optic chiasm, where the optic nerves criss-cross (close to the pituitary gland). For example, tumours of the pituitary gland often compress the optic nerve fibres and cause some degree of atrophy with loss of vision in that part of the visual field subserved by the fibres affected. Usually it is the fibres on the inner side of the optic nerve and those that cross at the chiasm that are most involved. These fibres supply the half of the retina nearer the nose, which receives images from the outer part of the visual field. Thus, in pituitary lesions it is common to find that the outer parts of both visual fields are abnormal, a condition called bitemporal hemianopia.

Certain chemicals, drugs, and nutritional deficiencies can also cause optic nerve damage or atrophy. If the underlying cause is corrected in time, some vision improvement may occur.

Optic Neuritis

Swelling of the optic nerve may be caused by inflammatory changes in the nerve, a condition known as optic neuritis. The inflammation causes a fairly rapid loss of vision in the affected eye, a new blind spot (a scotoma, usually in or near the centre of the visual field), pain in the eyeball (often occurring with eye movement), abnormal colour vision, and unusual flashes of light. The condition affects young to middle-aged people and affects women more often than men.

The optic nerve carries visual data from the retina of the eye to a relay station in the centre of the brain (the lateral geniculate nucleus) for transmission to a cortical area at the back of the brain (occipital lobes). Some instances of optic neuritis occur as a result of multiple sclerosis, a disease of unclear etiology that affects the optic nerve, brain, and spinal cord.

Such individuals may or may not have a previous history of neurologic problems, and further testing is often performed to investigate the potential diagnosis of multiple sclerosis. However, other manifestations of multiple sclerosis may not be fully evident until years after the onset of optic neuritis, if they occur at all. Other causes of optic neuritis include infections, such as Lyme disease or syphilis, as well as unknown causes, in which case the optic neuritis is termed idiopathic.

Optic neuritis may be centred in the optic disk, the point of exit of the nerve from the eye (papillitis), or it may be in the nerve shaft behind the eyeball (retrobulbar neuritis). The symptoms are loss of vision in or near the central part of the visual field, pain behind the eye, and pain when moving the eye. The optic nerve usually recovers from the inflammation, and vision gradually improves, but there often is residual degeneration of the nerve fibres and some persistence of visual symptoms. Repeated attacks of optic neuritis occur in some individuals.

OPTIC ATROPHY

Optic atrophy is the degeneration of the optic nerve due to direct or indirect damage to retinal ganglion cells, whose axonal projections collectively make up the optic nerve. Common causes of optic atrophy include glaucoma, tumours that press on the optic nerve, vascular (blood vessel) diseases, optic neuritis, trauma, and exposure to various drugs and toxins. The atrophy may be a hereditary defect, such as in Leber hereditary optic neuropathy (LHON), which predominantly affects males between the ages of 15 and 25. There is sometimes recovery of vision in LHON, but it is rarely complete. Treatment of optic atrophy is aimed at correcting the underlying condition to prevent further optic nerve damage.

GLAUCOMA

The thin coats of the eye are not sufficiently rigid in themselves to withstand distortion following the pull of the extraocular muscles when the eye is rotated. The eyeball is kept rigid by the action of the ciliary body, which secretes sufficient amounts of aqueous humour fluid to maintain the pressure of the eye at a level above atmospheric pressure. Aqueous humour is constantly being formed and drains away at the base of the iris through specialized drainage channels. Should these channels become blocked, the pressure within the eye rises to abnormally high levels. If the intraocular pressure remains raised for a long period of time, some retinal nerve fibres will atrophy, causing loss of visual function.

Glaucoma is the name given to a group of diseases that cause a particular type of optic neuropathy (i.e., optic nerve disease or abnormality) that results in visual field loss. Increased pressure within the eye is one of several important risk factors for development of glaucoma, but no one particular pressure is indicative of the disease. The susceptibility of an individual's optic nerve, and of the retinal cells whose fibres make up the optic nerve (ganglion cells), to damage at a particular eye pressure varies widely. Typically, a "normal" eye pressure range is between 10 and 21 mm (0.4 and 0.82 inch) of mercury, but glaucoma can arise in people with pressure below 21 mm (normal-tension glaucoma, or low-tension glaucoma). In addition, people with pressures above 21 mm (ocular hypertension) may never show signs or symptoms of glaucoma. A person's eye pressure is determined by the rate of aqueous humour formation by the ciliary body and the resistance to outflow through various pathways. Two major classes of glaucoma are primary open angle glaucoma (POAG) and angle closure glaucoma.

Primary open angle glaucoma is a common disease and a leading cause of vision loss in older individuals. Although the actual cause is not known, it may be due to degenerative changes in the outflow channels for aqueous fluid. It is rare below age 40, but after this its incidence increases. Genetic influences are important, and relatives of patients with glaucoma are more likely than others to develop the disease, as are individuals of African descent, who also tend to be affected more severely.

The symptoms of POAG are slight or absent in the early stages. The slow progressive optic nerve damage does not cause pain, and the early visual loss is in the peripheral parts of the visual field, affecting central vision only late in the disease. Both eyes are usually involved, although one may be more severely affected than the other. Since vision loss from glaucoma cannot be restored, successful treatment can only prevent further loss of vision. It is of great importance, therefore, that the disease be diagnosed as early as possible. Measurement of the intraocular pressure is of great value in the diagnosis of glaucoma. This is a simple test that can be applied as a screening method for surveys of the normal population.

The medical treatment of POAG consists of the use of eyedrops that lower the intraocular pressure. Inhibitors of the enzyme carbonic anhydrase, when taken by mouth, reduce the formation of aqueous humour and are used as an additional measure when necessary. If the pressure remains raised in spite of all medical treatment, then surgical methods or laser treatments must be used to increase the drainage of fluid from the eye. Treatments aimed at other potential mechanisms involved in glaucoma are under investigation.

Another common type of glaucoma is called angle closure glaucoma. It can be caused by mechanisms that either push the iris forward from behind or pull it forward to block the outflow of aqueous humour through the trabecular meshwork. The trabecular meshwork is located in the anterior chamber angle formed at the insertion (far periphery) of the iris. The aqueous fluid formed in the ciliary body behind the iris flows forward through the pupil

A scene as it might be viewed by a person with glaucoma. National Eye Institute, National Institutes of Health

to the angle of the anterior chamber. In one form of angle closure glaucoma, called pupillary block glaucoma, the lens seals against the iris and blocks the flow of aqueous humour through the pupil. The root of the iris (which is rather thin) is then pushed forward because of increased posterior pressure, which closes the angle and prevents outflow of aqueous humour. The angle may eventually become completely closed, causing intraocular pressure to rise rapidly. The eye then becomes red, hard, and painful, and vision deteriorates. The pain may be so severe as to cause vomiting. Urgent treatment is required to lower the pressure and prevent damage to the optic nerve that could lead to permanent vision loss.

In some cases an acute attack such as this heralds the onset of glaucoma; however, most people experience minor subacute attacks that are relieved by rest and usually reoccur over months or years. Medical and surgical treatments are usually effective in lowering the pressure in an acute attack and preventing recurrences. Other causes of glaucoma include chronic inflammatory disease of the eye, tumours within the eye, and congenital afflictions of the eye. Congenital glaucoma usually is found in the neonatal or infantile period and is heralded by tearing, aversion to light, eyelid spasms, and clouding and enlargement of the cornea. Treatment is aimed at medically or surgically reducing intraocular pressure, but long-term visual prognosis is often poor.

CHAPTER 8
VISUAL DISORDERS AND EYE INJURIES

Visual disorders encompass a wide range of conditions. Some examples include eyestrain, retinitis pigmentosa, night blindness, nearsightedness, farsightedness, colour blindness, and double vision. There are various causes of visual disorders; for example, some conditions arise secondary to preexisting disease, whereas others result from physical injury or are caused by inherited genetic defects. Many of these disorders, especially those arising from abnormalities in refraction (e.g., nearsightedness), are common and are easily corrected with the use of contact lenses or eyeglasses. However, treatments for some visual disorders, such as retinitis pigmentosa and colour blindness, are primarily supportive, rather than curative, and affected persons must learn to adapt to their visual impairments.

Among the more frequently occurring causes of temporary visual impairment are ocular injuries, despite the existence of protective mechanisms designed to prevent injury to the human eye. Such injuries often result from frontal impact to the eye socket or from the introduction of a foreign body into the eye. Though many of these conditions resolve with no long-term consequences to vision, some injuries can result in permanent vision loss.

VISUAL DISORDERS

FLOATERS, BLIND SPOTS, AND FLASHES

One of the most common visual symptoms is the sensation of small black objects floating in front of the eye, known as "floaters." These move with the eye but lag slightly at the beginning of an eye movement and overshoot when the movement stops. They are due to proteins, cells, and fragments of debris in the vitreous cavity of the eye. In certain conditions, as when looking at a blue sky, almost everybody can perceive them, and they are normal phenomena. However, a sudden increase in their number may indicate degenerative changes in the vitreous, which are particularly likely to occur in nearsighted individuals and in older people. These changes, although annoying, are of no serious import. The appearance of many floaters, however, may be associated with inflammation, bleeding in the eye, or a retinal tear and should be evaluated urgently.

Blind areas in the field of vision, called "blind spots," occasionally force people to seek medical advice. Any condition that causes failure of function of part of the retina, the optic nerve, or the optic pathway to the brain can cause such a blind spot, and the symptom requires careful investigation. There is a naturally occurring blind spot in each visual field that corresponds with the lack of retinal elements where the optic nerve leaves the eye. The brain is so skillful in filling in the visual pattern that the normal blind spot can be detected only by special methods.

Flashing lights in the field of vision are caused by stimulation of the retina by mechanical means. Most commonly this occurs when the vitreous degenerates and pulls slightly on its attachments to the retina. Similar symptoms also arise when the retina becomes torn or detached, causing brief flashing lights to be seen. The combination of the abrupt onset of multiple flashes and floaters with a sensation of a shadowy "curtain" or "veil" coming across the vision strongly suggests the presence of a retinal tear and detachment.

VISUAL FIELD DEFECT

A blind spot (scotoma) or blind area within the normal field of one or both eyes is known as a visual field defect. In most cases the blind spots or areas are persistent, but in some instances they may be temporary and shifting, as in the scotomata of migraine headache. The visual fields of the right and left eye overlap significantly, and visual field defects may not be evident without specific testing of each eye separately. Causes of visual field defects are numerous and include glaucoma, vascular disease, tumours, retinal disease, hereditary disease, optic neuritis and other inflammatory processes, nutritional deficiencies, toxins, and drugs.

Certain patterns of visual field loss help to establish a possible underlying cause. For instance, generalized constriction of the visual field can be due to glaucoma, retinitis pigmentosa, hysteria, or chronic high intracranial pressure. Increases in intracranial pressure can also cause enlargement of the natural blind spot due to abnormal swelling of the optic disks in both eyes, a condition called papilledema.

When defects occur in the visual field of only one eye, the cause can be localized to the eye or to anterior visual pathways (before the two optic nerves meet at the optic chiasm). In contrast, defects that involve the visual fields of both eyes often (but not always, as in the case of glaucoma) reflect disease processes at the optic chiasm or farther back in the brain. The specific condition where visual field defects are present in corresponding halves of the right and left eye fields is called homonymous hemianopia, whereas defects involving the outer or inner halves of both visual fields are called bitemporal or binasal hemianopia, respectively.

The extent and the location of the blind areas in the visual fields may provide further clues concerning the location of the lesion responsible. Bitemporal hemianopia suggests, for example, a lesion in the optic chiasm, the point at which the optic nerves from the two eyes meet and exchange some of the nerve fibres from each retina. A tumour of the pituitary may press upon the chiasm and have this effect. Precise demonstration of visual field defects can be accomplished via perimetry, in which the affected individual fixates his or her gaze straight ahead and indicates whether he or she can see special test lights projected onto an illuminated domed screen.

NYSTAGMUS

Nystagmus is characterized by involuntary back and forth, up and down, or circular movements of the eyes that are often described by observers as "jumping" or "dancing" eye movements. One type of nystagmus, called pendular nystagmus, is characterized by even, smooth eye movements, whereas in the type referred to as jerk nystagmus the movements are sharper and quicker in one direction than in the other. Jerk nystagmus can occur normally, such as when one is dizzy (e.g., from spinning around in circles) or is watching objects pass by quickly from the window of a moving vehicle. Pathologic nystagmus may be present at or shortly after birth because of retinal or optic nerve abnormalities, cataracts, albinism, or a host of other conditions (sensory nystagmus). Alternatively, people can be born with nystagmus and no associated abnormalities of the eye (congenital motor nystagmus). Often there is a gaze or a head position that the affected individual adopts in which the nystagmus is least severe and visual acuity is optimized (called the null point).

A subtype of nystagmus, called spasmus nutans, occurs in infants and is associated with head nodding and a twisted neck position (torticollis). Acquired childhood or adult nystagmus may be caused by intracranial tumours or other neurologic abnormalities, as well as certain vascular diseases, multiple sclerosis, drug intoxication, and metabolic disorders. Treatment consists of correcting any underlying ocular or neurologic causes of the nystagmus, if possible. In congenital nystagmus, the involuntary eye movements may be lessened by eyeglasses fitted with prisms or possibly by surgery to change the resting position of the eyes. Many people with nystagmus function well and do not require treatment.

DEFECTS OF LIGHT AND COLOUR PERCEPTION

Defective vision under reduced illumination may reflect the congenital or hereditary condition known as retinitis pigmentosa or may be acquired as a result of severe deficiency of vitamin A.

Defective colour vision affects men more often than women. Total colour blindness is extremely rare and is nearly always associated with poor vision in ordinary light and with nystagmus. Individuals who are partially colour-defective, such as those with red-green colour blindness, may not be aware of the disability until special instruments are used to test the person's ability to distinguish between hues in one or another part of the visible light spectrum. With these less-severe colour deficiencies, other visual functions are usually normal.

Retinitis Pigmentosa

Retinitis pigmentosa is a group of hereditary eye diseases in which progressive degeneration of the retina leads to severe impairment of vision. In the usual course of disease, the light-sensitive structures called rods—which are the visual receptors used in dim light—are destroyed early on, causing night blindness in youth. Over time, further atrophy of the retina and changes in the layer of supporting cells known as the pigment epithelium occur. Commonly the field of vision becomes constricted until the affected person sees objects as if looking through a tunnel.

In most cases, the course of disease is very slow, and progression to total blindness is uncommon. There are several hereditary patterns for retinitis pigmentosa, and multiple genetic defects responsible for the various forms of disease have been isolated. Treatment is largely supportive and aimed at optimizing remaining vision. There are several types of therapy under development for the treatment of retinitis pigmentosa. Among the most promising of these therapies are retinal implants, which have demonstrated some ability to restore perception of light and dark in several blind patients. A retinal implant consists of an electrode implanted at the back of the eye that receives signals from a transmitter and camera embedded in a pair of eyeglasses. When the electrode receives a signal, it generates an electrical response that stimulates the optic nerve, sending impulses to the brain and thereby enabling the perception of light patterns.

When retinitis pigmentosa is associated with congenital hearing loss, the condition is called Usher syndrome, which is the most common cause of combined blindness and deafness in the United States.

Night Blindness

Night blindness, also called nyctalopia, results from the failure of the eye to adapt promptly from light to darkness and is characterized by a reduced ability to see in dim light or at night. It occurs as a symptom of numerous congenital and inherited retinal diseases or as a result of vitamin A deficiency.

Congenital night blindness with or without myopia (nearsightedness) occurs either as a dominant, recessive, or sex-linked hereditary trait and usually remains stable throughout life. Night blindness developing during childhood or adolescence may be an early sign of retinitis pigmentosa. Vitamin A deficiency, which causes reduced photosensitivity of rhodopsin (a chromoprotein) in rod cells, causes night blindness that is usually not severe, and vision most often recovers when adequate levels of the vitamin are administered.

Colour Blindness

The inability to distinguish one or more of the three colours red, green, and blue is known as colour blindness. Most people with colour-vision problems have a weak colour-sensing system rather than a frank loss of colour sensation. In the retina, humans have three types of cones. One type absorbs light best in wavelengths of blue-violet and another in the wavelengths of green. The third type is most sensitive to longer wavelengths — more sensitive to red. Colour-blind persons may be blind to one, two, or all of the colours red, green, and blue. (Blindness to red is called protanopia; to green, deuteranopia; and to blue, tritanopia.) Red-blind persons are ordinarily unable to distinguish between red and green, while blue-blind persons cannot distinguish between blue and yellow. Green-blind persons are unable to see the green part of the spectrum.

Hereditary red-green colour blindness, which affects about 20 times as many males as females, is a sex-linked recessive characteristic. A woman must inherit the trait from both parents to be red-green colour-blind. A red-green colour-blind man and a woman of normal colour vision have daughters who have normal colour vision but are carriers of the trait—that is, the daughters may have red-green colour-blind sons and daughters who are carriers. The sons of a red-green colour-blind man and a woman with normal vision who themselves have normal vision are unable to pass the red-green colour-blind trait on to offspring. The son of a normal man and a carrier woman may be red-green colour-blind, and the daughter of such a union may be a carrier. Thus, red-green colour blindness tends to skip generations.

Acquired colour blindness is usually of the blue-yellow type and can be due to retinal diseases, glaucoma, or optic nerve diseases. Total colour blindness (achromatopsia) is an extremely rare congenital affliction that is typically associated with poor vision, nystagmus, and light sensitivity.

EYESTRAIN

Eyestrain, or asthenopia, is the term used to describe subjective symptoms of fatigue, discomfort, lacrimation (tearing), and headache following the use of the eyes. Such symptoms may result from intensive, prolonged close work. In people with perfectly normal eyes, eyestrain may indicate abnormalities of muscle balance or refractive errors. Eyestrain is more likely to be manifest during periods of fatigue or stress and is common among students studying for examinations. Refractive errors require correction, and muscle imbalance may require treatment. Psychological factors can be more important to address than physical factors.

REFRACTIVE ERRORS

In a normal eye, rays of light from distant objects come to a focus on the retina. In near vision the refractive power of the eye is increased by altering the shape of the lens (i.e., causing it to become thicker) to focus the image on the retina. This ability to alter the shape of the lens decreases with age until fine print cannot be read at a normal reading distance. This condition is known as presbyopia and usually becomes increasingly problematic after age 40. It is corrected by the use of convex lenses for reading.

In some eyes, rays of light from distant objects are not brought to a focus on the retina but are focused on a plane in front of the retina, as in myopia (nearsightedness), or behind the retina, as in hyperopia (farsightedness). In myopia, near objects are brought into focus on the retina but distant objects can be seen clearly only with the aid of concave lenses. In hyperopia, distant objects can sometimes be brought into focus by using the accommodative power of the lens, and in young people there is usually sufficient accommodation to enable them to see close up as well. The constant accommodative effort required, however, may result in problems such as asthenopia or esotropia, and the necessity for accommodating for distance can be overcome by wearing convex glasses.

Another type of refractive error is astigmatism. In this condition the refractive power of the eye varies in different axes, depending on the path the light takes through the cornea. This is due to the presence of nonuniform corneal curvature and results in the distortion of vision at all viewing distances. Astigmatism is a common condition and can be corrected with the use of cylindrical lenses in eyeglasses or contact lenses.

In general, refractive errors are easily corrected with glasses and are rarely accompanied by any serious disease of the eyes. However, hyperopia is a factor in the development of some kinds of strabismus and vision loss (amblyopia) in children, and high degrees of myopia may be associated with serious degenerative changes within the eye, particularly the retina.

Presbyopia

The loss of ability to focus the eye sharply on near objects as a result of the decreasing elasticity of the lens of the eye is known as presbyopia. The eye's ability to focus on near and far objects—the power of accommodation—depends upon two forces, the elasticity of the lens of the eye and the action of the ciliary muscle (a roughly ring-shaped muscle that encircles the lens and is attached to it by suspensory ligaments). When the ciliary muscle is relaxed, the ring enlarges away from the lens and the suspensory ligaments are tautened, flattening the lens into a shape suitable for viewing distant objects. When the muscle contracts, the ligaments are loosened, and, because of the elasticity of the lens, the surface of the lens—particularly the front surface—becomes more curved, in keeping with viewing near objects. Ordinarily the lens gradually becomes less elastic (it hardens) with age, so the power of accommodation is lost progressively. The loss is most rapid after age 40, when most people become aware of difficulty in performing a task, such as reading, that requires near focusing; this can be helped with corrective lenses.

Accommodation may also be lost temporarily as a result of paralysis of the ciliary muscle. With this paralysis, which can occur from the action of certain toxins and medications, the muscle cannot contract, and the surface of the lens is prevented from becoming more convex.

Nearsightedness

Myopia, also called nearsightedness, is a visual abnormality in which the resting eye focuses the image of a distant object at a point in front of the retina, resulting in a blurred image.

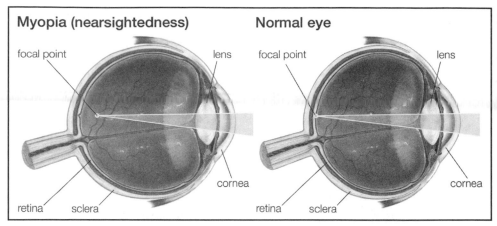

Myopia, or nearsightedness, can be corrected with glasses that have concave lenses to allow near objects to be brought into focus by the eye. Encyclopædia Britannica, Inc.

Myopic eyes, which are usually longer than normal from front to rear, are somewhat more susceptible to retinal detachment than are normal or farsighted eyes. Severe myopia can be associated with other eye problems as well, most of which affect the retina or the choroid (i.e., pathologic blood vessel growth from the choroid).

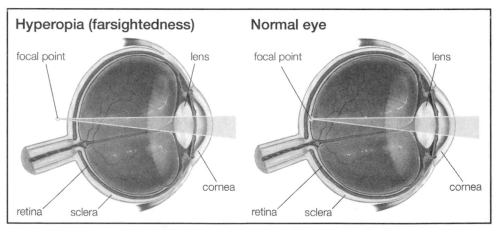

Hyperopia, or farsightedness, can be corrected with glasses that contain convex lenses to reduce the accommodative effort required for the eye to bring an object into focus. Encyclopædia Britannica, Inc.

Myopia can be corrected by concave lenses. Today, however, the use of LASIK (laser-assisted in situ keratomileusis) surgery has become common. LASIK surgery is often preferred to photorefractive keratectomy (PRK), another type of laser-based surgery used to reshape the cornea.

Farsightedness

Hyperopia, also called farsightedness, is a refractive error or abnormality in which the cornea and lens of the eye focus the image of the visual field at an imaginary point behind the retina. The retina thus receives an unfocused image of near objects, though distant objects may be in focus. Hyperopia frequently occurs when an eye is shorter than normal from front to rear; the lens is then unable to increase its convexity sufficiently to focus the images of close objects onto the retina. Corrective lenses for hyperopia are designed to supply the additional convexity needed for focusing. Hyperopic laser in situ keratomileusis (H-LASIK) and photorefractive keratectomy for hyperopia (H-PRK) are common surgical methods that reshape the cornea to improve vision in hyperopic patients.

Astigmatism

Astigmatism is a nonuniform curvature of the cornea that causes the eye to focus images at different distances, depending on the orientation of light as it strikes the cornea. The effect of astigmatism can also be produced by abnormalities or misalignment of the crystalline lens (sometimes called lenticular astigmatism), although this is rare. The portions of the image that are not focused on the retina (the light-sensitive tissue lining the inside of the eyeball) appear blurred. Astigmatism occurs independent of the existence of nearsightedness or farsightedness.

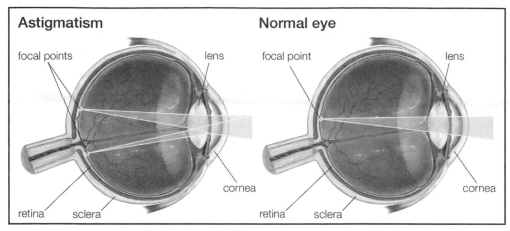

Astigmatism results from a nonuniform curvature of the cornea that produces distorted vision. This condition is often corrected with eyeglasses or contact lenses that contain a cylindrical lens. Encyclopædia Britannica, Inc.

This condition usually can be corrected through a precisely designed lens (eyeglasses or some forms of contact lenses) that counteracts the underlying corneal asymmetry. Refractive surgery is also capable of correcting limited amounts of astigmatism in some situations.

A troublesome form of astigmatism, "irregular" astigmatism, can be caused by corneal scars and certain corneal diseases and is sometimes seen after corneal transplant. If significant, visual impairment from irregular astigmatism can be difficult to treat, although rigid contact lenses may help.

VISION LOSS AND EYE MISALIGNMENT

BLINDNESS

Blindness is a transient or permanent inability to see any light at all (total blindness) or to retain any useful vision despite attempts at vision enhancement (functional blindness). Less-severe levels of vision impairment have been categorized, ranging from near-normal vision to various degrees of low vision to near-blindness, depending on the visual acuity and functional impact stemming from the vision loss. Legal blindness is a government-defined term that determines eligibility for various services or benefits as well as restrictions on certain activities such as driving.

Specific causes of impaired vision are too numerous to list. In general, any process that causes malfunction of the retina, the optic nerve, or the visual centres and pathways of the brain can reduce vision. In severe cases, blindness may result. Broad categories of conditions that impair vision include infections (e.g., gonorrhea or congenital rubella infection), inflammations (e.g., uveitis), congenital or hereditary diseases (e.g., retinitis pigmentosa), tumours, cataracts, trauma or mechanical injury, metabolic and nutritional disorders, glaucoma, vascular damage (e.g., diabetic eye disease or atherosclerosis), and refractive errors (e.g., nearsightedness or farsightedness). In addition, there are many vision-lowering conditions for which there is no well-understood cause (e.g., age-related macular degeneration).

Many other potentially blinding disorders do not fit easily into general categories. Few of these conditions, however, lead to total blindness, and many of them have some form of available treatment. Even when the underlying problem cannot be corrected, multiple low-vision aids have been developed to optimize remaining vision. In cases of functional or total blindness, other senses and skills must be emphasized or developed. In addition, a strong psychosocial support system can greatly enhance a person's ability to cope with vision loss.

DOUBLE VISION

Double vision, also called diplopia, is the perception of two images of a single object. Normal binocular vision results from the brain's fusion of slightly different images from each eye, with points on the retina of each eye corresponding to points on the retina of the opposite eye. Binocular diplopia occurs when the eyes are not properly aligned, and the image of an object that projects onto one retina does not fall spatially to the matching point on the other retina. In such a situation, the double image is eliminated when either eye is covered. It is commonly caused by temporary or permanent paralysis or restriction of one or more of the external eye muscles. The orientation of the double image is determined by the particular muscle (sometimes more than one muscle) that is not working properly.

Causes of binocular diplopia include myasthenia gravis, inflammatory processes, thyroid eye disease (Graves ophthalmopathy), small blood vessel disease (e.g., diabetes mellitus), trauma, infections, and various tumours. These processes usually induce diplopia by impairing the external eye muscles themselves or the nerves that directly or indirectly control their function. However, an underlying cause of diplopia is not always found. Frank displacement of the eyeball, via large orbital fractures or a mass pressing on the eyeball, can also cause double vision.

The treatment for binocular double vision varies depending on the cause, severity, and duration. Many cases of diplopia resolve on their own and require only temporary patching of one eye to eliminate the offending second image. People with permanent diplopia may benefit from prisms placed in eyeglasses or from surgical realignment of the eyes. Of course, treatment of underlying diseases or injuries is also essential.

Misalignment of the eyes in early childhood is a special situation. It usually does not result in symptomatic diplopia, as the child's developing brain suppresses the second image. Without correction, this often leads to amblyopia and permanent vision loss in the "suppressed" eye.

Monocular diplopia differs from binocular diplopia in that the double vision remains present when the nonaffected eye is covered. Monocular diplopia is due to abnormalities in the structure of the eyeball itself, most notably the lens and cornea. Treatment is directed at correcting the abnormality.

OPHTHALMOPLEGIA

Ophthalmoplegia, also called extraocular muscle palsy, occurs as a result of paralysis of the extraocular muscles that control the movements of the eye. Ophthalmoplegia usually involves the third (oculomotor), fourth (trochlear), or sixth (abducens) cranial nerves. Double vision is the characteristic symptom in all three cases. In oculomotor paralysis the muscles controlling the eye are affected in such a way that the eye drifts outward and slightly downward and has difficulty turning inward and upward. In addition, the upper eyelid of the affected eye usually droops, a condition called ptosis, and the pupil may be enlarged. If the pupil is abnormally large, the possibility of a cerebral aneurysm arises. This can be associated with pain. Trochlear paralysis, involving another muscle, the superior oblique, causes a vertical deviation of the affected eye. Abducens nerve paralysis affects still another ocular muscle, the lateral rectus, such that the affected eye turns inward toward the nose and cannot fully turn outward.

Ophthalmoplegia can be caused by congenital abnormalities, trauma, complications of viral infections, or

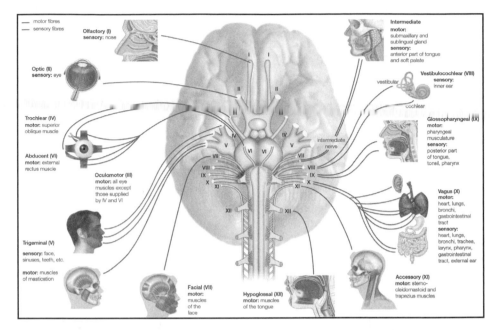

There are 12 pairs of cranial nerves that function to control the muscles and sense organs of the head and thoracic region. Several of these, including the third, fourth, and sixth nerves, control muscles that move the eye. Encyclopædia Britannica, Inc.

disorders that affect the nervous system, including multiple sclerosis, cerebral tumours, migraines, and vascular (blood vessel) disease such as that associated with diabetes. Ophthalmoplegia can also occur as a complication of muscle disorders such as myasthenia gravis, although it is usually associated with other muscular symptoms.

Treatment of ophthalmoplegia is directed at correcting any underlying disorders, if possible. In many cases, isolated nerve palsies resolve on their own over time, and treatment consists of patching the affected eye to alleviate any transient double vision. Eyeglasses fitted with prisms or surgical intervention may be helpful for people with long-standing ophthalmoplegia.

AMBLYOPIA

Amblyopia is a reduction in vision in one or both eyes due to abnormal visual experience in early childhood. Amblyopia can lead to functional changes in the visual centres of the brain. These changes result from eye-related problems that degrade or distort images received by the brain. The most common causes are misalignment of the eyes (strabismus) and uncorrected (usually asymmetric) refractive errors (e.g., farsightedness, nearsightedness, or astigmatism). Other conditions that affect the clarity of vision, such as congenital cataracts, can also cause amblyopia. In each of these situations the brain receives inferior or inappropriate visual information, which it suppresses over time.

If left untreated, these changes within the visual centres of the brain will become permanent and lead to irreversible vision deficits. Fortunately, this outcome is usually avoidable or reversible during early childhood by promptly correcting the underlying eye problem (removing the cataract or prescribing eyeglasses) or forcing the use of the weaker eye, often by carefully covering the stronger eye with a patch. However, despite the availability of effective treatments, amblyopia remains a major cause of childhood-onset reduced vision. Vision screening is an essential means of identifying children at risk of developing amblyopia.

STRABISMUS

Misalignment of the eyes is called strabismus, or squint. The deviant eye may be directed inward toward the other eye (cross-eye, or esotropia), outward, away from the other eye (exotropia), upward (hypertropia), or downward (hypotropia). The deviation is called "concomitant" if it remains constant in all directions of gaze and "incomitant" if the degree of misalignment varies with the direction of gaze.

Strabismus can be present all the time, intermittently, or brought out only by special testing. Congenital, or infantile, strabismus appears in infancy and is presumably due to defects present at birth that are poorly understood. However, given the strong tendency for strabismus to run in families, the causes undoubtedly have some genetic component. While congenital strabismus is more common in children with birth-related problems, most affected children are otherwise neurologically normal. Acquired strabismus appears later in life and has many potential etiologies. For example, acquired strabismus can be due to diseases or trauma affecting the actual muscles responsible for moving the eye or the nerves or brain stem centres controlling those muscles. In addition, poor vision in one or both eyes can lead to sensory strabismus, in which the eye with the poorest vision drifts slightly over time. In children, a common contributor to acquired strabismus is farsightedness (hyperopia), which, when severe enough, can secondarily cause the eyes to cross as the child tries to focus on an object (accommodative esotropia).

The chief danger of strabismus in early childhood is monocular vision loss, or amblyopia, a condition that can become permanent if not treated promptly. If the brain receives two separate images because of the presence of a consistently deviating eye, the less-used eye may develop amblyopia as a result of suppression of the unwanted second image. Often in the treatment of strabismus, the preferred ("better-seeing") eye is patched for a period of time to encourage the child to use the "weaker" eye and thereby improve the weaker eye's vision. Patching therapy is effective at younger ages but is generally not useful in older teenagers and adults. Thus, early identification and treatment of amblyopia are critical.

Depending on the situation, important nonsurgical treatments for strabismus may include correcting any underlying nearsightedness (myopia), farsightedness (hyperopia), or astigmatism with eyeglasses or fitting glasses with prisms. However, definitive treatment commonly requires surgical manipulation of one or more muscles that control eye movement in an effort to realign the two eyes.

OCULAR INJURIES

The bony orbit provides excellent protection for the eye, especially from blunt injuries. A blow to the front of the orbit with a rounded instrument such as a fist or a tennis ball, however, can cause a shock wave to travel through the eye, damaging many structures along the way, including the retina. Central vision may be reduced after such injuries without any obvious changes in the appearance of the eye. In severe cases the bones of the orbit may be fractured. Perforating wounds from glass, sharp metal fragments, and so on are always serious. Injuries to the lens can result in the formation of a cataract, and often after penetrating injuries the eye remains inflamed for a considerable time.

One rare type of inflammation following injury, called sympathetic ophthalmia, is of particular importance. In this condition an injured eye causes the other, previously normal eye to take part in the inflammation, with resulting impairment of vision. Sympathetic ophthalmia can occur weeks, months, or years after the initial injury. The cause of sympathetic ophthalmia is not fully known, but if an injured eye is removed within 10 days of injury, sympathetic ophthalmia almost never occurs in the other eye. In the past there was little effective treatment for the condition, but therapy with corticosteroids and other immunomodulatory agents has proved effective in controlling inflammation in many cases.

FOREIGN BODIES

Most foreign bodies that contact the eye remain on or near the surface. When they touch the cornea, they cause intense pain and a flow of tears. The tears may be sufficient to wash the foreign body out of the eye, but, if it becomes embedded in the cornea, it may have to be removed surgically. Many small foreign bodies lodge in the undersurface of the upper lid in such a way that every time the eye blinks, the foreign body rubs on the cornea, causing pain and irritation. Metallic foreign bodies embedded in the cornea often leave rust rings, which should be removed to aid in proper healing.

Small foreign bodies traveling at high speeds may penetrate into the interior of the eye with remarkably few symptoms, and their presence may not be recognized until weeks or months later when inflammatory changes occur. The most common foreign bodies to enter the eye in this way are fragments of metal from hammer-and-chisel accidents or from moving parts of machinery. Whenever such injuries are suspected, it is important to locate the position of the fragment as carefully as possible and to remove it by surgery. If the foreign body is magnetic, a magnet can be used to attract the foreign body to the site of entry into the eye, permitting extraction. Safety goggles or glasses equipped with safety lenses are of utmost importance in the prevention of such accidents during high-risk activities.

CHEMICAL AND RADIATION INJURIES

Strong acids and alkalis cause severe injury if they contact the eye. Alkalis, such as lye, ammonia, and lime, are particularly damaging in that they tend to rapidly melt and penetrate the cornea, producing extensive tissue destruction within the eye. Speed is the vital factor in first-aid treatment, and copious irrigation with water is the first essential step. Delay of first-aid treatment in the hope of finding a neutralizing substance is a serious error, as strong acids and alkalis quickly become bound to the ocular tissues and cause severe damage.

Except for extremely intense light, such as that from a laser or from prolonged staring at the Sun, the visible wavelengths of the electromagnetic spectrum—i.e., visible light rays—rarely cause ocular injury. Retinal damage from staring at the Sun causes visual impairment that often improves after months, although residual deficits can remain. Ultraviolet light (UV), however, is strongly absorbed by the cornea surface and is the cause of a condition known as snow blindness (so called because it can occur in skiers from UV light reflected off snow) and a closely related condition called arc eye (also called welder's flash; caused by the intense flash of UV light produced when using a welding rod). Symptoms, consisting of intense pain and copious flow of tears, may not occur until some time after exposure. Treatment consists of temporary eye patching and application of cold compresses and soothing artificial lubricants to the eye. Usually the eyes recover without any permanent damage.

Extensive exposure to ionizing radiation, without adequate protection for the eyes, can cause cataract formation as well as corneal and conjunctival damage. The lens is also susceptible to X-rays, and the eyes require shielding when therapeutic irradiation is used for growths around or near the eye.

COMPLICATIONS OF SYSTEMIC DISEASE

THE CENTRAL NERVOUS SYSTEM

Since the optic nerve and retina are, embryonically, an extension of the brain, it is not surprising that central nervous system diseases frequently affect the eye. As a result, visual defects may be the earliest evidence of general nervous system disease. The nerve supply to the ocular muscles, particularly the extraocular muscles, may also be involved early in some diseases of the central nervous system. This will result in defective movement of the eyes, causing lack of coordination between the two eyes and diplopia, or double vision.

The nerve fibres that connect the retina with the site of primary visual sensation in the occipital cortex (part of the occipital lobe, located in the rear of the brain) travel across the brain in a regular pattern, and many lesions of the brain, such as tumours, impinge on part of this pathway. From a detailed examination of the sensitivity of different parts of the retina (visual field testing), it is often possible to localize the site of an intracranial lesion. A frequent first symptom of multiple sclerosis is sudden onset of loss of central vision in one eye caused by optic neuritis. Detailed ophthalmic examination is therefore essential in any patient suspected of having disease of the central nervous system.

ARTERIOSCLEROSIS AND HYPERTENSION

The eye is the one structure in the body in which the blood vessels are easily visible to the examiner. Changes observed in the retinal vessels mirror changes that are taking place in other parts of the body, particularly those in the brain. In arteriosclerosis, degenerative changes occur in the walls of arteries that lead to thickening of arterial walls and narrowing of blood vessels and may give rise to complete occlusion (blockage) of a vessel. If the central retinal artery that supplies blood to the inner retina is affected, loss of vision is profound and sudden and, unless the obstruction can be relieved right away, permanent. Occlusion of the retinal veins is more common than arterial occlusion and also has dramatic effects caused by the damming up of blood in the eye. Blockage of retinal veins results in the bursting of small vessels, retinal swelling, and multiple hemorrhages scattered over the retina. Some degree of recovery of vision is usual but depends on whether a branch of the central vein or the central vein itself is occluded.

Vascular hypertension, or raised blood pressure, usually occurs in association with arteriosclerosis. Typical changes can be recognized in the small vessels of the fundus (the back portion of the interior of the eyeball). In severe cases, multiple hemorrhages, exudates (leaking proteinaceous fluid), and swelling of the optic disk (the head of the optic nerve) may be present. As with arteriosclerosis, hypertension can lead to vascular occlusions of the retina. The presence of hypertension typically worsens the effects of diabetic eye disease in patients having both afflictions.

DIABETES

Diabetic eye disease is a major cause of vision loss and blindness. It occurs more commonly with increasing duration of the disease and increasing patient age. People with advanced diabetic retinal disease are at increased risk of heart, kidney, and peripheral vascular disease. The actual cause of the changes in the retinal vessels is not clear, but the natural history of the disease is well recognized. Two general types of diabetic eye disease are known and are characterized as nonproliferative diabetic retinopathy (which lacks abnormal blood vessel growth) and proliferative diabetic retinopathy (in which abnormal blood vessels are present in the retina and sometimes the iris). Each type possesses different levels of severity, although one common cause of vision loss in diabetes, macular edema, can occur in either type at any level of severity. Nonproliferative diabetic retinopathy features changes due to damaged, weakened blood vessels, in which tiny aneurysms form and small hemorrhages and swelling within the retina can be seen. Areas of retinas that no longer receive appropriate blood flow, a condition called ischemia, can also appear. Visual loss at this stage may be absent or caused by retinal swelling or ischemia. If unchecked, nonproliferative diabetic retinopathy can lead to worsened blood flow to the retina, more severe damage, and the appearance of new abnormal blood vessels on the optic disk, retina, and even iris (proliferative diabetic retinopathy). Changes in these abnormal vessels can cause hemorrhage into the vitreous cavity, retinal detachment, and glaucoma.

Prevention or control of diabetic retinopathy relies on control of blood glucose levels. Various types of laser photocoagulation of the retina are used in certain forms of diabetic retinopathy in an attempt to halt or slow its progression. In cases of retinal detachment or persistent or recurrent hemorrhage within the vitreous gel, more extensive surgical treatments are employed. Glaucoma stemming from diabetic eye disease is often difficult to treat, but both medical and surgical approaches can be attempted.

THYROID DISEASE

Graves ophthalmopathy (an eye disease related to thyroid dysfunction) usually occurs in people with hyperthyroidism, although it can occur in people with normal or even reduced thyroid function. It is characterized by swelling and inflammation of the orbital tissues, including the extraocular muscles, that may lead to retraction of the eyelids, restriction of eye movement (causing double vision), and bulging forward of the eyeball (called exophthalmos, or proptosis). Although exophthalmos arises primarily from inflammation, the associated processes of cellular proliferation and accumulation of fluid in the tissues that surround the eyeball in its socket, or orbit, also are important pathological processes underlying its development. The swelling of tissues in Graves ophthalmopathy can also cause pressure on the optic nerve behind the eyeball, leading to vision loss. In most uncomplicated situations treatment is conservative, relying only on artificial lubrication, but in severe cases the lids may need to be partially sutured together or surgery may be required to relieve pressure in the orbit. Further eye muscle and lid surgeries may also be needed to correct persistent eye problems related to Graves ophthalmopathy.

EXOPHTHALMOS

In addition to Graves ophthalmopathy, other causes of exophthalmos include other orbital inflammatory conditions, spread of infection from the paranasal sinuses or teeth, trauma, various orbital tumours, and vascular (blood vessel) abnormalities of the orbit. It should also be noted that "prominent" eyes can be a normal inherited trait in certain families.

Exophthalmos often leads to increased exposure of the eye surface, which can produce irritation and redness. Other symptoms or findings that can coincide with exophthalmos include eyelid swelling or retraction, deep orbital pain, and double vision. In severe cases, vision can be threatened from exposure-induced cornea damage or compression of the optic nerve within the orbit. Treatment of symptomatic exophthalmos is directed at correcting any underlying disorders (e.g., hyperthyroidism), as well as providing lubrication of the eye surface, if necessary. Persistent exophthalmos from Graves ophthalmopathy can be managed with medication, surgery, or radiation therapy. Vision loss or vision-threatening changes associated with exophthalmos require prompt intervention.

RHEUMATOID ARTHRITIS

The ocular complications of rheumatoid arthritis involve the sclera and cornea and can cause dry eye. Inflammation of the sclera, called scleritis, can cause intense, boring pain and, if severe, could be associated with life-threatening systemic disease. Treatment varies, depending on the disease severity, but generally includes anti-inflammatory and immune-modulating agents.

CHAPTER 9

DIAGNOSIS
AND TREATMENT
OF EYE DISEASES

The modern field of ophthalmology was borne from centuries of observation and discovery that eventually became grounded in scientific knowledge. A significant advance in the understanding and diagnosis of eye diseases was the development in the 19th century of the ophthalmoscope, an instrument for inspecting the interior of the eye. With this device, ophthalmologists could readily examine the retina and its blood vessels, thereby obtaining valuable information about the inner eye and eye diseases.

Since the development of the ophthalmoscope, a number of important advances in the diagnosis and treatment of eye diseases have occurred. Included among these advances are eye exams, treatments, and eye banks to store corneas for transplants. Ophthalmologists also have designed tests for visual function that enable them to more precisely identify and diagnose eye diseases. In addition, today there exist several different types of corrective lenses and surgeries tailored for the treatment of specific visual disorders. These treatments have successfully restored vision to normal or near-normal in countless people worldwide.

OPHTHALMOLOGY

Ophthalmology is the medical specialty dealing with the diagnosis and treatment of diseases and disorders of

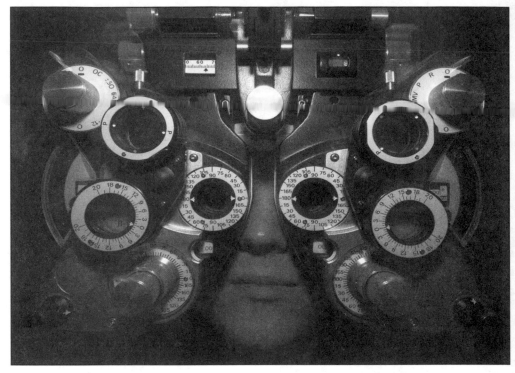

Phoropter used during an eye examination. U.S. Navy (Image Number: 040305-N-4190W-001)

the eye. The first ophthalmologists were known as oculists. These paramedical specialists practiced on an itinerant basis during the Middle Ages. Georg Bartisch, a German physician who wrote on eye diseases in the 16th century, is sometimes credited with founding the medical practice of ophthalmology. Many important eye operations were first developed by oculists, as, for example, the surgical correction of strabismus, first performed in 1738. The first descriptions of visual defects included those of glaucoma (1750), night blindness (1767), colour blindness (1794), and astigmatism (1801).

The first formal course in ophthalmology was taught at the medical school of the University of Göttingen in 1803, and the first medical eye clinic with an emphasis on teaching, the London Eye Infirmary, was opened in 1805, initiating the modern specialty. Advances in optics by the Dutch physician Frans Cornelis Donders in 1864 established the modern system of prescribing and fitting eyeglasses to a particular vision problem. The invention of the ophthalmoscope for looking at the interior of the eye created the possibility of relating eye defects to internal medical conditions.

In the 20th century, advances in the field chiefly involved the prevention of eye disease through regular eye examinations and the early treatment of congenital eye defects. Another major development was the eye bank, first established in 1944 in New York, which made corneal tissues for transplantation more generally available. Other 20th-century advances included the refinement of contact lenses and the development of corrective surgeries such as LASIK (laser-assisted in situ keratomileusis).

Ophthalmologists are concerned with whatever adversely affects vision, whether such adverse events are caused by faulty development of the eye, disease, injury, degeneration, senescence, or refraction. An ophthalmologist performs tests of visual function and examines the interior of the eye as part of a general physical examination for symptoms of systemic or neurologic diseases. He or she also prescribes medical treatment for eye diseases and glasses for refraction and performs surgical operations where indicated.

OPTOMETRY

Optometry is a health-care profession concerned with examining the eyes for defects of vision and diagnosing and treating such conditions. Optometrists prescribe and supply eyeglasses, contact lenses, and other optical aids that correct the focusing of the eyes. They also examine the eyes to detect such disorders as glaucoma and cataracts. In addition, optometrists counsel people on the correct use and care of the eyes, supervise exercise and training programs that are designed to treat problems of vision, and help rehabilitate patients who have low or severely restricted vision. Unlike the ophthalmologist, who is a physician with a specialization in the diagnosis and treatment of eye diseases (and who may also test vision and prescribe corrective lenses), the optometrist generally is not trained to perform surgery. In some areas, however, optometrists are licensed to use topical therapeutic drugs and to treat glaucoma and other eye diseases with systemic drugs.

Requirements for the practice of optometry vary. In the United States professional optometrists must complete a four-year course of study in addition to two to four years of undergraduate work and must be licensed by the state in which they practice. Schools of optometry are accredited nationally by the Council on Optometric Education and grant the Doctor of Optometry (O.D.) degree.

The optician, another optical specialist, makes, fits, and sells optical devices, particularly the corrective lenses prescribed by optometrists and ophthalmologists.

OPHTHALMOSCOPE

The ophthalmoscope is an instrument for inspecting the interior of the eye. It was invented in 1850 by German scientist and philosopher Hermann von Helmholtz. The ophthalmoscope became a model for later forms of endoscopy. The device consists of a strong light that can be directed into the eye by a small mirror or prism. The light reflects off the retina and back through a small hole in the ophthalmoscope, through which the examiner sees a non-stereoscopic magnified image of the structures at the back of the eye, including the optic disk, retina, retinal blood vessels, macula, and choroid. The ophthalmoscope is particularly useful as a screening tool for various ocular diseases, such as diabetic retinopathy.

OPHTHALMOLOGICAL EXAMINATION

An ophthalmological examination includes a thorough history, with a particular focus on a patient's symptoms. The ophthalmologist physically examines the eyes with special devices and does various tests to determine visual function. The most important subjective test is for visual acuity. This is usually performed by having the patient read, from a set distance, an eye chart with a series of letters of graded sizes, which become increasingly smaller as the chart is read from top to bottom. The person is asked to read the lowest line legible, and visual acuity is then expressed in terms of the size of the letter and the distance at which it is read, relative to a person with normal vision.

The visual field can be assessed by many methods. The confrontation visual field exam is the most basic test and involves a simple assessment of peripheral vision. In this test one eye of the patient is covered, the ophthalmologist presents one or more fingers in the peripheral visual field, and the patient indicates the number of fingers displayed. The Goldmann visual field exam is another manual test, in which the patient focuses straight ahead on a central point while an object is moved inward from the periphery. The ophthalmologist performs this several times, testing different areas of the visual field and drawing a map of the visual field for each eye. Another technique, called automated perimetry, uses a bowl-shaped instrument into which the patient looks, focusing on a central point. The instrument sends out random computer-generated flashes of light of varying durations, intensities, and locations that may or may not be within the patient's visual field. When the patient sees a flash, he or she presses a button, sending a signal that is automatically detected and incorporated into a map of the patient's visual field. Automated visual field testing is commonly used today, especially in assessing glaucoma.

Other subjective examinations include colour vision testing and tests of visual perception under reduced illumination. Examination of the external eye and part of the anterior segment is facilitated by the use of a binocular microscope attached to a slit lamp (a variable source of light that projects the image of a slit onto the eye). The direct and indirect ophthalmoscope has an

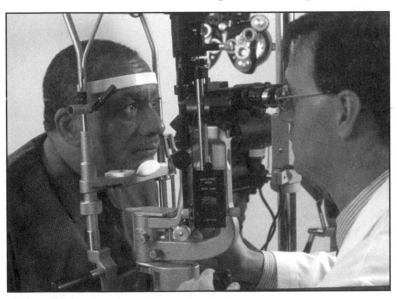

This eye care professional uses the high magnification of a slit lamp to examine a patient's eyes. National Eye Institute, National Institutes of Health

illuminating system that lights up the interior of the eye and a viewing system through which the fundus can be observed. Photography of the anterior part of the eye and of the fundus is also widely used.

Other specialized methods of examination include examination of the angle of the anterior chamber by means of a specially designed mirrored contact lens (goniolens), which is used in conjunction with the slit-lamp microscope. The electrical responses of the retina and brain to light entering the eye can also be recorded and are of great value in certain conditions.

Estimation of the intraocular pressure is an important part of an ophthalmological examination and is accomplished by an instrument called a tonometer. This instrument is designed specifically to measure the tension or pressure that exists within the eyeball. Many types of tonometers are used, each of which has unique advantages and disadvantages.

The refractive state of the eye can be measured objectively or subjectively or by a combination of methods. The simplest method is subjective, using lenses of different powers to give a trial-and-error estimate of the best correcting lenses. More accurate results can be obtained by using an instrument known as a retinoscope, which gives an objective assessment of the refraction that can subsequently be modified by subjective methods to suit the individual requirements of the patient.

Many other tools are used to examine the eye and aid in the diagnosis of eye diseases, including ultrasound, retinal angiography, and devices to measure corneal curvature and topography. New devices and techniques are constantly being introduced, advancing the eye care specialist's ability to diagnose and treat eye disorders.

OPTICAL AIDS

The most widely used optical aids are eyeglasses (spectacles), and the technical design of eyeglass lenses has advanced considerably. A simple biconcave or biconvex lens causes considerable vision distortion if objects are viewed through the periphery of the lens, but, if the back surface of the lens is made concave and the required power is attained by altering the curvature of the front surface, improvement in peripheral vision results. Modern eyeglass lenses are of this form.

Most older people require an additional lens for reading, which can be incorporated with the distance correction in the form of a bifocal lens. In some occupations an intermediate distance is also required, and a third segment can be added, forming a trifocal lens. The complete range of correction from distance to near can be achieved by means of a progressive lens, in which lens power increases as the eye moves downward, with the upper segment of the lens providing the correction for distance and the lowest segment of the lens representing the reading correction. By slightly tilting the head, it is possible to find the optimum correction for intermediate distances.

The distortion of peripheral view when using conventional eyeglasses occurs because the correcting lens does not move when the eye moves. This problem can be completely overcome by the use of contact lenses, which fit the anterior surface of the cornea and thus move with the eye. The earliest types were larger than the cornea and were uncomfortable to wear, but the development of smaller "hard" lenses greatly increased the scope and usefulness of contact lenses. Even so, the length of time for which they could be worn was limited until rigid gas (oxygen)-permeable lenses were introduced, which allow oxygen to pass through to the cornea much more effectively. Flexible "soft" lenses, made of water-absorbing plastic gel, also allow oxygen to reach the surface of the cornea reasonably well. The type of contact lens that best suits an individual is dependent upon the refraction and any coexisting corneal problems.

For those persons who cannot obtain useful vision with ordinary eyeglasses or contact lenses, much can still be done through the use of special lens systems known as low-vision aids. These devices provide a magnified image but reduce the visual field. Their main value is to enable a person to read normal print that would otherwise be difficult to read. They can be of use for distance, particularly when viewing conditions are relatively static, as with the cinema, theatre, or television. Large-print materials, video magnifiers, closed-circuit television, and optimal lighting and contrast conditions are also of great benefit. For those with profound or complete vision loss, enhancement of other skills that help substitute for vision is crucial to optimizing function.

EYEGLASSES

Eyeglasses are lenses set in frames for wearing in front of the eyes to aid vision or to correct such defects of vision as myopia, hyperopia, and astigmatism. In 1268 English philosopher and scientist Roger Bacon made the earliest recorded comment on the use of lenses for optical purposes, but magnifying lenses inserted in frames were used for reading both in Europe and China at this time, and it is a matter of controversy whether the West learned from the East or vice versa. In Europe eyeglasses first appeared in Italy, their introduction being attributed to Alessandro di Spina of Florence. The first portrait to show eyeglasses is that of Hugh of Provence by Tommaso da Modena, painted in 1352. In 1480 Domenico Ghirlandaio painted St. Jerome at a desk from which dangled eyeglasses; as a result, St. Jerome became the patron saint of the spectacle-makers' guild. The earliest glasses had convex lenses to aid farsightedness. A concave lens for myopia, or nearsightedness, is first evident in the portrait of Pope Leo X painted by Raphael in 1517.

In 1784 American author, scientist, and statesman Benjamin Franklin invented bifocals, dividing his lenses for distant and near vision, the split parts being held together by the frame. Cemented bifocals were invented in 1884, and the fused and one-piece types followed in 1908 and 1910, respectively. Trifocals and new designs in bifocals were later introduced, including the Franklin bifocal revived in one-piece form.

Originally, lenses were made of transparent quartz and beryl, but increased demand led to the adoption of optical glass, for which Venice and Nürnberg were the chief centres of production. In 1885 German physicist Ernst Abbe and German chemist Otto Schott demonstrated that the incorporation of new elements into the glass melt led to many desirable variations in refractive index and dispersive power. In the modern process, glass for lenses is first rolled into plate form. Most lenses are made from clear crown glass of refractive index 1.523. In high myopic corrections, a cosmetic improvement is effected if the lenses are made of dense flint glass (refractive index 1.69) and coated with a film of magnesium fluoride to nullify the surface reflections. Flint glass, or barium crown, which has less dispersive power, is used in fused bifocals. Plastic lenses have become increasingly popular, particularly if the weight of the lenses is a problem, and plastic lenses are more shatterproof than glass ones. In sunglasses, the lenses are tinted to reduce light transmission and to avoid glare.

CONTACT LENSES

A contact lens is a thin, artificial lens worn on the surface of the eye to correct refractive defects of vision. The first contact lens, made of glass, was developed in 1887 by German physiologist Adolf Fick to correct irregular astigmatism. The early lenses, however, were uncomfortable and could not be worn for long. Until the development of optical instruments that could measure the curvature of the cornea, the contact lens was made by taking an impression of the eye and fashioning a lens on a mold.

Contact lenses most effectively neutralize visual defects arising from irregular curvatures of the cornea. They are the preferred treatment for some varieties of astigmatism and aphakia (absence of the eye's crystalline lens). They also can be functionally and cosmetically appealing substitutes for eyeglasses to treat myopia (near-sightedness) and other visual defects.

In the mid-1900s, plastic-based contact lenses were designed that rested on a cushion of tears on the cornea, covering the area over the iris and pupil. These older hard-plastic contact lenses had a limited wearing time because of potential irritation of the cornea, and they required a period of adaptation when first worn. Both front and back surfaces of the hard contact lens are spherically curved, altering refractive properties by changing the shape of the tear film on the eye's surface, which conforms to the curve of the rear surface of the contact lens, and by a difference in curvature between the two surfaces of the lens itself. In the 1970s, gas-permeable rigid contact lenses were developed that allowed much more oxygen to pass through to the corneal surface, thus increasing comfort and wear time.

Also in the 1970s, larger "soft" lenses, made from a water-absorbing plastic gel for greater flexibility, were introduced. Soft contact lenses are usually comfortable because they allow oxygen to penetrate to the eye's surface. Their large size makes them more difficult to lose than hard lenses. Their delicacy, however, makes them more subject to damage, and, as with all contact lenses, they require careful maintenance. They are less effective than hard lenses in treating astigmatism, because they reflect the underlying corneal curvature more closely. In 2005 hybrid lenses were developed that are gas-permeable and rigid and surrounded by a soft ring. These lenses provide the comfort of a soft lens with the visual sharpness of a hard lens.

Contact lenses have particular advantages in treating certain defects that can be corrected only partially by prescription eyeglasses; for example, contact lenses avoid the distortion of size that occurs with thick corrective lenses. However, most contact lenses cannot be worn overnight, as this significantly increases the risk of serious corneal infections. Contact lenses can also be used in certain situations to protect the corneal surface during healing and to relieve discomfort derived from corneal surface problems.

CORRECTIVE SURGERY

LASIK

LASIK, or laser-assisted in situ keratomileusis, is a laser-based eye surgery commonly used to correct nearsightedness, farsightedness, and astigmatism. LASIK eye surgery was developed in the early 1990s, when ophthalmologists combined the technique of keratomileusis, in which the cornea is removed, frozen, reshaped, and replaced, with the technique of photorefractive keratectomy (PRK), in which a laser is used to reshape the cornea. In the LASIK procedure a hinged flap is made in the outer corneal tissue and lifted out of the way to allow an excimer laser (an ultraviolet chemical lascr, also called an exciplex laser) to reshape the underlying tissue. Tissue reshaping improves the eye's ability to focus light and thus relieves blurred vision and reduces dependency on eyeglasses or contact lenses. The natural adherence properties of the replaced corneal flap negate the need for stitches. LASIK surgery is often preferred to photorefractive keratectomy.

PHOTOREFRACTIVE KERATECTOMY

Photorefractive keratectomy, or PRK, is a common surgical method that reshapes the cornea to improve vision in patients affected by farsightedness or nearsightedness. In this procedure a local anesthetic is applied to the eye and a laser beam is used to sculpt the cornea. Reshaping enables the cornea to focus light on the retina, which it cannot do in hyperopic or myopic eyes.

PRK differs from other laser-based eye surgeries such as LASIK in that it is not an invasive surgery; no incisions are made in the cornea during PRK. However, because a significant amount of corneal tissue is damaged during the reshaping process, the amount of time needed for recovery following PRK is longer relative to LASIK. In addition, patients often experience some discomfort during the healing process. Improvement in vision is often noticeable within several days after surgery, although optimal vision may not occur for several months.

RADIAL KERATOTOMY

Radial keratotomy, or RK, is a surgical procedure to correct nearsightedness. The technique was first developed by Russian eye surgeon Svyatoslav Nikolay Fyodorov in the 1970s. In the 1980s and early 1990s, RK was a widespread procedure for correcting nearsightedness, with several hundred thousand procedures performed worldwide. It has since been replaced by laser-based refractive surgeries, such as PRK and LASIK, that offer improved image quality and outcome predictability.

The cornea contributes approximately 66 percent of the focusing power of the eye. In cases of nearsightedness the focusing ability of the cornea is too strong, resulting in blurred vision. RK reduces this focusing power by surgically flattening the corneal curvature, resulting in sharper vision. In the RK procedure the surgeon makes a series of incisions in the cornea in a spokelike pattern. The incision depth is approximately 90 percent of the corneal thickness. A central "hub" is left uncut in the cornea. The RK incisions emanate radially outward from this hub. The incisions weaken the cornea's mechanical strength, resulting in a flattened shape and reduced refractive power. Modulating the size of the hub and the number of incisions controls the amount of corneal flattening. Side effects of RK include progressive corneal flattening leading to farsightedness and starburst patterns attributed to diffraction from the surgical scars encroaching on the eye's pupil.

CONCLUSION

The human eye remains an important subject of modern science. In fact, the study of the human eye encompasses a far more diverse area of research in the 21st century than ever before. Molecular and cell biologists continue to investigate the eye at its most basic level, studying its cells and biochemical processes, to better understand how all the components of the eye function together. Likewise, doctors and scientists conducting clinical research are developing new drugs and therapeutic approaches to treat the numerous different kinds of eye diseases.

Among the most promising recent developments in eye research are those related to advances in scientists' knowledge of stem cells. New laboratory technologies have enabled scientists to reprogram skin cells into stem cells, which have the potential to develop into any kind of cell in the human body. Studies conducted in animals have shown that mature cells can be reprogrammed into eye cells, such as those of the cornea and retina; these cells can then be transplanted into corresponding diseased tissues in the eye. Scientists are hopeful that such stem cell therapies will eventually be made available for the treatment of human eye diseases such as retinitis pigmentosa.

In recent years there also have occurred significant advancements in gene therapy, in which a normal gene is inserted into an individual's genome in order to repair a mutation that causes a genetic disease. This technology is being investigated for the treatment of hereditary blinding conditions such as macular degeneration. Major breakthroughs such as stem cell and gene therapy are the culmination of decades of scientific research into the basic processes of cell and eye function. Though a great deal of research still is needed to ensure that these new therapeutic approaches are effective and safe, they represent vital progress and indicate that treatments for some of the most common and progressive eye diseases will be made available in the near future.

GLOSSARY

asthenopia Eyestrain often caused by psychological factors, the symptoms of which include fatigue, headache, tearing, and discomfort.

axon Part of a neuron that connects to other neurons or cells and transports impulses away from the cell body.

bipolar cell A type of neuron in the retina that is connected to ganglions on one end and either one cone cell or multiple rod cells on the other end.

concave lens A lens that curves inward, like a bowl.

cone Cone-shaped light-sensing cell in the retinas of vertebrates that processes colour and detail and converts light into impulses to the optic nerve fibre.

convex lens A rounded lens that curves outward, like a sphere.

dendrite Part of a neuron that typically transports impulses toward a cell body.

diplopia Double vision, or perceiving two images of a single object, resulting from the projection of an object's image onto non-corresponding locations on the retina of each eye.

emmetropia Condition in which light rays focus directly on the retina, resulting in normal vision.

ganglion cell A type of neuron in the retina that receives input from both rods and cones.

hyperopia Farsightedness resulting from the image of a visual field focusing behind the retina.

innervate To provide an organ with nerves.

luminosity Brightness or intensity of light projected by a source.

mesopic vision Eyesight in medium lighting that is facilitated by both the rods and cones of the retina.

myopia Nearsightedness resulting from the image of a visual field focusing in front of the retina.

nodule Tissue or cells that have amassed into a hard, protruding growth.

ophthalmology Field of medicine concerned specifically with the afflictions and treatment of the eye.

optic chiasm X-shaped structure below the hypothalamus where half the optic nerve fibres from each eye cross over to join nerve fibres from the opposite eye on the opposite side of the brain. The remaining half of the fibres continue on the same respective side of the brain.

orbit Hollow in the skull for the eye; eye socket.

photopic vision Eyesight in bright light that is facilitated by the cones of the retina.

presbyopia Loss of elasticity in the eye lens that results in the inability to focus on nearby objects.

quantum A small unit of radiant energy, equivalent to the product of Planck's constant and the frequency of the radiation.

refraction Change in a wave's direction caused by its passage through a different medium and the resultant change in the wave's velocity.

rod Rod-shaped light-sensing cell in the retinas of vertebrates that converts stimuli from photons into electrical and chemical stimuli for the nervous system.

saccade Rapid eye movement, often accompanied by a head movement, that shifts the gaze so that the fovea can take in the various aspects of a visual field.

scotoma Blind spot or area of the visual field in which vision is severely limited.

scotopic vision Eyesight in low light that is facilitated by the rods of the retina.

stereopsis Depth perception resulting from the projection of an object's image, as it is perceived by each eye, to a single hemisphere of the brain.

torsion Rotation of an organ on its own axis.

visual field Everything visible to a stationary eye at a given moment.

Bibliography

Detailed information about the human eye, eye diseases, and the field of ophthalmology can be found in Gary H. Cassel, Michael D. Billig, and Harry G. Randall, *The Eye Book: A Complete Guide to Eye Disorders and Health* (1998); Daniel M. Albert and Frederick A. Jakobiec (eds.), *Principles and Practice of Ophthalmology*, 2nd ed., 6 vol. (2000); and Daniel M. Albert and Diane D. Edwards, *The History of Ophthalmology* (1996). A monumental ongoing series covering all aspects of sensory reception in organisms is Hansjochem Autrum (ed.), Handbook of Sensory Physiology (1971–). An introductory work pertaining specifically to photoreception is Robert W. Rodieck, The First Steps in Seeing (1998). The optical systems of eyes are discussed in relation to their role in vision in a wide range of organisms in Jerome J. Wolken, Light Detectors, Photoreceptors, and Imaging Systems in Nature (1995); and Michael F. Land and Dan-Eric Nilsson, Animal Eyes (2002). The types and functions of eye movements are covered in Roger H.S. Carpenter, Movements of the Eyes, 2nd ed. (1988). An appealing work on the basic aspects of the different eye structures and the mechanisms of photoreception specific to invertebrates is Eric Warrant and Dan-Eric Nilsson, Invertebrate Vision (2006). Information on the structure and photoreception mechanisms of the human eye is provided in Clyde W. Oyster, The Human Eye: Structure and Function (1999). An excellent general text is Robert Sekuler and Randolph Blake, Perception, 5th ed. (2005), focusing on perception through the senses. Irvin Rock, An Introduction to Perception (1975), is an introductory text in experimental psychology.

INDEX

J

jerk nystagmus, 189
Jerome, St., 222

K

keratitis, 160–162, 163
keratoconjunctivitis, 153, 154, 160, 161
keratoconus, 164
keratomileusis, 224

L

lacrimal (tear) ducts and glands, 43, 48–49, 54, 56, 145–146, 161
lacrimal pump, 56
lacrimal sac, 48, 56, 145
lacrimal secretions (tears), 22, 44, 48–49, 53, 54–56
lacrimation, 48, 56, 158, 159, 185, 193, 206, 207
lactic acid, 39–40
lamellae of corneal stroma, 23
lamina cribrosa, 26
lamina fusca, 26
Landolt C, 89
laser-assisted in situ keratomileusis (LASIK) surgery, 197, 215, 224–225
laser photocoagulation of retina, 210–211
LASIK surgery, 197, 215, 224–225
lateral geniculate bodies, 31, 35, 39, 112, 119, 120–122, 180
lateral geniculate neurons, 92, 112, 140–141
lateral palpebral raphe, 46

Leber hereditary optic neuropathy (LHON), 181
legal blindness, 199
length comparison estimation, 128–129
lens, artificial, 170, 171, 172
lens, crystalline, 17, 19, 20, 21, 29, 39, 41, 42, 66–74, 168, 169–172, 193–194, 195, 197, 205, 208
lens capsule, 42, 68, 70, 169
lenses, contact, 69, 160, 164, 171, 172, 186, 194, 198, 215, 220–221, 223–224, 225
lenticular astigmatism, 197
leukoma, 24
levator aponeurosis, 46
levator palpebral muscles, 46, 47, 51–52, 151, 152
LHON (Leber hereditary optic neuropathy), 181
light absorption, 82–83, 113, 114–115
light-adapted eye/retina, 78, 102, 108, 109
light detection threshold, 78, 79–81, 83–86
light diffraction, 93
light-insensitive layers, 32
light intensity, 85
light path in eye, 28, 29, 32–33, 94
light perception defects, 190–192
light protection, 47, 53
light reflex, 71–74, 121
light sensitivity
  of retina, 79, 80, 81, 86–87, 92–93
  as symptom, 159, 160, 167, 185, 193

P